Leading Edge Trends for AI Driverless Cars

Practical Innovations in
Artificial Intelligence and Machine Learning

Dr. Lance B. Eliot, MBA, PhD

Disclaimer: This book is presented solely for educational and entertainment purposes. The author and publisher are not offering it as legal, accounting, or other professional services advice. The author and publisher make no representations or warranties of any kind and assume no liabilities of any kind with respect to the accuracy or completeness of the contents and specifically disclaim any implied warranties of merchantability or fitness of use for a particular purpose. Neither the author nor the publisher shall be held liable or responsible to any person or entity with respect to any loss or incidental or consequential damages caused, or alleged to have been caused, directly or indirectly, by the information or programs contained herein. Every company is different and the advice and strategies contained herein may not be suitable for your situation.

DEDICATION

To my incredible daughter, Lauren, and my incredible son, Michael.

Forest fortuna adiuvat (from the Latin; good fortune favors the brave).

CONTENTS

ACKNOWLEDGMENTS

I have been the beneficiary of advice and counsel by many friends, colleagues, family, investors, and many others. I want to thank everyone that has aided me throughout my career. I write from the heart and the head, having experienced first-hand what it means to have others around you that support you during the good times and the tough times.

To Warren Bennis, one of my doctoral advisors and ultimately a colleague, I offer my deepest thanks and appreciation, especially for his calm and insightful wisdom and support.

To Mark Stevens and his generous efforts toward funding and supporting the USC Stevens Center for Innovation.

To Lloyd Greif and the USC Lloyd Greif Center for Entrepreneurial Studies for their ongoing encouragement of founders and entrepreneurs.

To Peter Drucker, William Wang, Aaron Levie, Peter Kim, Jon Kraft, Cindy Crawford, Jenny Ming, Steve Milligan, Chis Underwood, Frank Gehry, Buzz Aldrin, Steve Forbes, Bill Thompson, Dave Dillon, Alan Fuerstman, Larry Ellison, Jim Sinegal, John Sperling, Mark Stevenson, Anand Nallathambi, Thomas Barrack, Jr., and many other innovators and leaders that I have met and gained mightily from doing so.

Thanks to Ed Trainor, Kevin Anderson, James Hickey, Wendell Jones, Ken Harris, DuWayne Peterson, Mike Brown, Jim Thornton, Abhi Beniwal, Al Biland, John Nomura, Eliot Weinman, John Desmond, and many others for their unwavering support during my career.

And most of all thanks as always to Michael and Lauren, for their ongoing support and for having seen me writing and heard much of this material during the many months involved in writing it. To their patience and willingness to listen.

INTRODUCTION

This is a book that provides the newest innovations and the latest Artificial Intelligence (AI) advances about the emerging nature of AI-based autonomous self-driving driverless cars. Via recent advances in Artificial Intelligence (AI) and Machine Learning (ML), we are nearing the day when vehicles can control themselves and will not require and nor rely upon human intervention to perform their driving tasks (or, that <u>allow</u> for human intervention, but only *require* human intervention in very limited ways).

Similar to my other related books, which I describe in a moment and list the chapters in the Appendix A of this book, I am particularly focused on those advances that pertain to self-driving cars. The phrase "autonomous vehicles" is often used to refer to any kind of vehicle, whether it is ground-based or in the air or sea, and whether it is a cargo hauling trailer truck or a conventional passenger car. Though the aspects described in this book are certainly applicable to all kinds of autonomous vehicles, I am focused more so here on cars.

Indeed, I am especially known for my role in aiding the advancement of self-driving cars, serving currently as the Executive Director of the Cybernetic Self-Driving Cars Institute.. In addition to writing software, designing and developing systems and software for self-driving cars, I also speak and write quite a bit about the topic. This book is a collection of some of my more advanced essays. For those of you that might have seen my essays posted elsewhere, I have updated them and integrated them into this book as one handy cohesive package.

You might be interested in companion books that I have written that provide additional key innovations and fundamentals about self-driving cars. Those books are entitled **"Introduction to Driverless Self-Driving Cars," "Advances in AI and Autonomous Vehicles: Cybernetic Self-Driving Cars," "Self-Driving Cars: "The Mother of All AI Projects," "Innovation and Thought Leadership on Self-Driving Driverless Cars," "New Advances in AI Autonomous Driverless Self-Driving Cars," and "Autonomous Vehicle Driverless Self-Driving Cars and**

Artificial Intelligence" and **"Transformative Artificial Intelligence Driverless Self-Driving Cars,"** and **"Disruptive Artificial Intelligence and Driverless Self-Driving Cars,** and **"State-of-the-Art AI Driverless Self-Driving Cars,"** and **"Top Trends in AI Self-Driving Cars,"** and **"AI Innovations and Self-Driving Cars,"** **"Crucial Advances for AI Driverless Cars,"** **"Sociotechnical Insights and AI Driverless Cars,"** and **"Pioneering Advances for AI Driverless Cars"** (they are all available via Amazon). See Appendix A of this herein book to see a listing of the chapters covered in those three books.

For the introduction here to this book, I am going to borrow my introduction from those companion books, since it does a good job of laying out the landscape of self-driving cars and my overall viewpoints on the topic. The remainder of the book is all new material that does not appear in the companion books.

INTRODUCTION TO SELF-DRIVING CARS

This is a book about self-driving cars. Someday in the future, we'll all have self-driving cars and this book will perhaps seem antiquated, but right now, we are at the forefront of the self-driving car wave. Daily news bombards us with flashes of new announcements by one car maker or another and leaves the impression that within the next few weeks or maybe months that the self-driving car will be here. A casual non-technical reader would assume from these news flashes that in fact we must be on the cusp of a true self-driving car.

Here's a real news flash: We are still quite a distance from having a true self-driving car. It is years to go before we get there.

Why is that? Because a true self-driving car is akin to a moonshot. In the same manner that getting us to the moon was an incredible feat, likewise can it be said for achieving a true self-driving car. Anybody that suggests or even brashly states that the true self-driving car is nearly here should be viewed with great skepticism. Indeed, you'll see that I often tend to use the word "hogwash" or "crock" when I assess much of the decidedly *fake news* about self-driving cars. Those of us on the inside know that what is often reported to the outside is malarkey. Few of the insiders are willing to say so. I have no such hesitation.

Indeed, I've been writing a popular blog post about self-driving cars and hitting hard on those that try to wave their hands and pretend that we are on the imminent verge of true self-driving cars. For many years, I've been known as the AI Insider. Besides writing about AI, I also develop AI software. I do what I describe. It also gives me insights into what others that are doing AI are really doing versus what it is said they are doing.

Many faithful readers had asked me to pull together my insightful short essays and put them into another book, which you are now holding in your hands.

For those of you that have been reading my essays over the years, this collection not only puts them together into one handy package, I also updated the essays and added new material. For those of you that are new to the topic of self-driving cars and AI, I hope you find these essays approachable and informative. I also tend to have a writing style with a bit of a voice, and so you'll see that I am times have a wry sense of humor and also like to poke at conformity.

As a former professor and founder of an AI research lab, I for many years wrote in the formal language of academic writing. I published in referred journals and served as an editor for several AI journals. This writing here is not of the nature, and I have adopted a different and more informal style for these essays. That being said, I also do mention from time-to-time more rigorous material on AI and encourage you all to dig into those deeper and more formal materials if so interested.

I am also an AI practitioner. This means that I write AI software for a living. Currently, I head-up the Cybernetics Self-Driving Car Institute, where we are developing AI software for self-driving cars. I am excited to also report that my son, also a software engineer, heads-up our Cybernetics Self-Driving Car Lab. What I have helped to start, and for which he is an integral part, ultimately he will carry long into the future after I have retired. My daughter, a marketing whiz, also is integral to our efforts as head of our Marketing group. She too will carry forward the legacy now being formulated.

For those of you that are reading this book and have a penchant for writing code, you might consider taking a look at the open source code available for self-driving cars. This is a handy place to start learning how to develop AI for self-driving cars. There are also many new educational courses spring forth.

There is a growing body of those wanting to learn about and develop self-driving cars, and a growing body of colleges, labs, and other avenues by which you can learn about self-driving cars.

This book will provide a foundation of aspects that I think will get you ready for those kinds of more advanced training opportunities. If you've already taken those classes, you'll likely find these essays especially interesting as they offer a perspective that I am betting few other instructors or faculty offered to you. These are challenging essays that ask you to think beyond the conventional about self-driving cars.

THE MOTHER OF ALL AI PROJECTS

In June 2017, Apple CEO Tim Cook came out and finally admitted that Apple has been working on a self-driving car. As you'll see in my essays, Apple was enmeshed in secrecy about their self-driving car efforts. We have only been able to read the tea leaves and guess at what Apple has been up to. The notion of an iCar has been floating for quite a while, and self-driving engineers and researchers have been signing tight-lipped Non-Disclosure Agreements (NDA's) to work on projects at Apple that were as shrouded in mystery as any military invasion plans might be.

Tim Cook said something that many others in the Artificial Intelligence (AI) field have been saying, namely, the creation of a self-driving car has got to be the mother of all AI projects. In other words, it is in fact a tremendous moonshot for AI. If a self-driving car can be crafted and the AI works as we hope, it means that we have made incredible strides with AI and that therefore it opens many other worlds of potential breakthrough accomplishments that AI can solve.

Is this hyperbole? Am I just trying to make AI seem like a miracle worker and so provide self-aggrandizing statements for those of us writing the AI software for self-driving cars? No, it is not hyperbole. Developing a true self-driving car is really, really, really hard to do. Let me take a moment to explain why. As a side note, I realize that the Apple CEO is known for at times uttering hyperbole, and he had previously said for example that the year 2012 was "the mother of all years," and he had said that the release of iOS 10 was "the mother of all releases" – all of which does suggest he likes to use the handy "mother of" expression. But, I assure you, in terms of true self-driving cars, he has hit the nail on the head. For sure.

When you think about a moonshot and how we got to the moon, there are some identifiable characteristics and those same aspects can be applied to creating a true self-driving car. You'll notice that I keep putting the word "true" in front of the self-driving car expression. I do so because as per my essay about the various levels of self-driving cars, there are some self-driving cars that are only somewhat of a self-driving car. The somewhat versions are ones that require a human driver to be ready to intervene. In my view, that's not a true self-driving car. A true self-driving car is one that requires no human driver intervention at all. It is a car that can entirely undertake via automation the driving task without any human driver needed. This is the essence of what is known as a Level 5 self-driving car. We are currently at the Level 2 and Level 3 mark, and not yet at Level 5.

Getting to the moon involved aspects such as having big stretch goals, incremental progress, experimentation, innovation, and so on. Let's review how this applied to the moonshot of the bygone era, and how it applies to the self-driving car moonshot of today.

Big Stretch Goal

Trying to take a human and deliver the human to the moon, and bring them back, safely, was an extremely large stretch goal at the time. No one knew whether it could be done. The technology wasn't available yet. The cost was huge. The determination would need to be fierce. Etc. To reach a Level 5 self-driving car is going to be the same. It is a big stretch goal. We can readily get to the Level 3, and we are able to see the Level 4 just up ahead, but a Level 5 is still an unknown as to if it is doable. It should eventually be doable and in the same way that we thought we'd eventually get to the moon, but when it will occur is a different story.

Incremental Progress

Getting to the moon did not happen overnight in one fell swoop. It took years and years of incremental progress to get there. Likewise for self-driving cars. Google has famously been striving to get to the Level 5, and pretty much been willing to forgo dealing with the intervening levels, but most of the other self-driving car makers are doing the incremental route. Let's get a good Level 2 and a somewhat Level 3 going. Then, let's improve the Level 3 and get a somewhat Level 4 going. Then, let's improve the Level 4 and finally arrive at a Level 5. This seems to be the prevalent way that we are going to achieve the true self-driving car.

Experimentation

You likely know that there were various experiments involved in perfecting the approach and technology to get to the moon. As per making incremental progress, we first tried to see if we could get a rocket to go into space and safety return, then put a monkey in there, then with a human, then we went all the way to the moon but didn't land, and finally we arrived at the mission that actually landed on the moon. Self-driving cars are the same way. We are doing simulations of self-driving cars. We do testing of self-driving cars on private land under controlled situations. We do testing of self-driving cars on public roadways, often having to meet regulatory requirements including for example having an engineer or equivalent in the car to take over the controls if needed. And so on. Experiments big and small are needed to figure out what works and what doesn't.

Innovation

There are already some advances in AI that are allowing us to progress toward self-driving cars. We are going to need even more advances. Innovation in all aspects of technology are going to be required to achieve a true self-driving car. By no means do we already have everything in-hand that we need to get there. Expect new inventions and new approaches, new algorithms, etc.

Setbacks

Most of the pundits are avoiding talking about potential setbacks in the progress toward self-driving cars. Getting to the moon involved many setbacks, some of which you never have heard of and were buried at the time so as to not dampen enthusiasm and funding for getting to the moon. A recurring theme in many of my included essays is that there are going to be setbacks as we try to arrive at a true self-driving car. Take a deep breath and be ready. I just hope the setbacks don't completely stop progress. I am sure that it will cause progress to alter in a manner that we've not yet seen in the self-driving car field. I liken the self-driving car of today to the excitement everyone had for Uber when it first got going. Today, we have a different view of Uber and with each passing day there are more regulations to the ride sharing business and more concerns raised. The darling child only stays a darling until finally that child acts up. It will happen the same with self-driving cars.

SELF-DRIVING CARS CHALLENGES

But what exactly makes things so hard to have a true self-driving car, you might be asking. You have seen cruise control for years and years. You've lately seen cars that can do parallel parking. You've seen YouTube videos of Tesla drivers that put their hands out the window as their car zooms along the highway, and seen to therefore be in a self-driving car. Aren't we just needing to put a few more sensors onto a car and then we'll have in-hand a true self-driving car? Nope.

Consider for a moment the nature of the driving task. We don't just let anyone at any age drive a car. Worldwide, most countries won't license a driver until the age of 18, though many do allow a learner's permit at the age of 15 or 16. Some suggest that a younger age would be physically too small to reach the controls of the car. Though this might be the case, we could easily adjust the controls to allow for younger aged and thus smaller stature. It's not their physical size that matters. It's their cognitive development that matters.

To drive a car, you need to be able to reason about the car, what the car can and cannot do. You need to know how to operate the car. You need to know about how other cars on the road drive. You need to know what is allowed in driving such as speed limits and driving within marked lanes. You need to be able to react to situations and be able to avoid getting into accidents. You need to ascertain when to hit your brakes, when to steer clear of a pedestrian, and how to keep from ramming that motorcyclist that just cut you off.

Many of us had taken courses on driving. We studied about driving and took driver training. We had to take a test and pass it to be able to drive. The point being that though most adults take the driving task for granted, and we often "mindlessly" drive our cars, there is a significant amount of cognitive effort that goes into driving a car. After a while, it becomes second nature. You don't especially think about how you drive, you just do it. But, if you watch a novice driver, say a teenager learning to drive, you suddenly realize that there is a lot more complexity to it than we seem to realize.

Furthermore, driving is a very serious task. I recall when my daughter and son first learned to drive. They are both very conscientious people. They wanted to make sure that whatever they did, they did well, and that they did not harm anyone. Every day, when you get into a car, it is probably around 4,000 pounds of hefty metal and plastics (about two tons), and it is a lethal weapon. Think about it. You drive down the street in an object that weighs two tons and with the engine it can accelerate and ram into anything you want to hit. The damage a car can inflict is very scary. Both my children were surprised that they were being given the right to maneuver this monster of a beast that could cause tremendous harm entirely by merely letting go of the steering wheel for a moment or taking your eyes off the road.

In fact, in the United States alone there are about 30,000 deaths per year by auto accidents, which is around 100 per day. Given that there are about 263 million cars in the United States, I am actually more amazed that the number of fatalities is not a lot higher. During my morning commute, I look at all the thousands of cars on the freeway around me, and I think that if all of them decided to go zombie and drive in a crazy maniac way, there would be many people dead. Somehow, incredibly, each day, most people drive relatively safely. To me, that's a miracle right there. Getting millions and millions of people to be safe and sane when behind the wheel of a two ton mobile object, it's a feat that we as a society should admire with pride.

So, hopefully you are in agreement that the driving task requires a great deal of cognition. You don't' need to be especially smart to drive a car, and we've done quite a bit to make car driving viable for even the average dolt. There isn't an IQ test that you need to take to drive a car. If you can read and write, and pass a test, you pretty much can legally drive a car. There are of course some that drive a car and are not legally permitted to do so, plus there are private areas such as farms where drivers are young, but for public roadways in the United States, you can be generally of average intelligence (or less) and be able to legally drive.

This though makes it seem like the cognitive effort must not be much. If the cognitive effort was truly hard, wouldn't we only have Einstein's that could drive a car? We have made sure to keep the driving task as simple as we can, by making the controls easy and relatively standardized, and by having roads that are relatively standardized, and so on. It is as though Disneyland has put their Autopia into the real-world, by us all as a society agreeing that roads will be a certain way, and we'll all abide by the various rules of driving.

A modest cognitive task by a human is still something that stymies AI. You certainly know that AI has been able to beat chess players and be good at other kinds of games. This type of narrow cognition is not what car driving is about. Car driving is much wider. It requires knowledge about the world, which a chess playing AI system does not need to know. The cognitive aspects of driving are on the one hand seemingly simple, but at the same time require layer upon layer of knowledge about cars, people, roads, rules, and a myriad of other "common sense" aspects. We don't have any AI systems today that have that same kind of breadth and depth of awareness and knowledge.

As revealed in my essays, the self-driving car of today is using trickery to do particular tasks. It is all very narrow in operation. Plus, it currently assumes that a human driver is ready to intervene. It is like a child that we have taught to stack blocks, but we are needed to be right there in case the child stacks them too high and they begin to fall over. AI of today is brittle, it is narrow, and it does not approach the cognitive abilities of humans. This is why the true self-driving car is somewhere out in the future.

Another aspect to the driving task is that it is not solely a mind exercise. You do need to use your senses to drive. You use your eyes a vision sensors to see the road ahead. You vision capability is like a streaming video, which your brain needs to continually analyze as you drive. Where is the road? Is there a pedestrian in the way? Is there another car ahead of you? Your senses are relying a flood of info to your brain. Self-driving cars are trying to do the same, by using cameras, radar, ultrasound, and lasers. This is an attempt at mimicking how humans have senses and sensory apparatus.

Thus, the driving task is mental and physical. You use your senses, you use your arms and legs to manipulate the controls of the car, and you use your brain to assess the sensory info and direct your limbs to act upon the controls of the car. This all happens instantly. If you've ever perhaps gotten something in your eye and only had one eye available to drive with, you suddenly realize how dependent upon vision you are. If you have a broken foot with a cast, you suddenly realize how hard it is to control the brake pedal and the accelerator. If you've taken medication and your brain is maybe sluggish, you suddenly realize how much mental strain is required to drive a car.

An AI system that plays chess only needs to be focused on playing chess. The physical aspects aren't important because usually a human moves the chess pieces or the chessboard is shown on an electronic display. Using AI for a more life-and-death task such as analyzing MRI images of patients, this again does not require physical capabilities and instead is done by examining images of bits.

Driving a car is a true life-and-death task. It is a use of AI that can easily and at any moment produce death. For those colleagues of mine that are developing this AI, as am I, we need to keep in mind the somber aspects of this. We are producing software that will have in its virtual hands the lives of the occupants of the car, and the lives of those in other nearby cars, and the lives of nearby pedestrians, etc. Chess is not usually a life-or-death matter.

Driving is all around us. Cars are everywhere. Most of today's AI applications involve only a small number of people. Or, they are behind the scenes and we as humans have other recourse if the AI messes up. AI that is driving a car at 80 miles per hour on a highway had better not mess up. The consequences are grave. Multiply this by the number of cars, if we could put magically self-driving into every car in the USA, we'd have AI running in the 263 million cars. That's a lot of AI spread around. This is AI on a massive scale that we are not doing today and that offers both promise and potential peril.

There are some that want AI for self-driving cars because they envision a world without any car accidents. They envision a world in which there is no car congestion and all cars cooperate with each other. These are wonderful utopian visions.

They are also very misleading. The adoption of self-driving cars is going to be incremental and not overnight. We cannot economically just junk all existing cars. Nor are we going to be able to affordably retrofit existing cars. It is more likely that self-driving cars will be built into new cars and that over many years of gradual replacement of existing cars that we'll see the mix of self-driving cars become substantial in the real-world.

In these essays, I have tried to offer technological insights without being overly technical in my description, and also blended the business, societal, and economic aspects too. Technologists need to consider the non-technological impacts of what they do. Non-technologists should be aware of what is being developed.

We all need to work together to collectively be prepared for the enormous disruption and transformative aspects of true self-driving cars. We all need to be involved in this mother of all AI projects.

WHAT THIS BOOK PROVIDES

What does this book provide to you? It introduces many of the key elements about self-driving cars and does so with an AI based perspective. I weave together technical and non-technical aspects, readily going from being concerned about the cognitive capabilities of the driving task and how the technology is embodying this into self-driving cars, and in the next breath I discuss the societal and economic aspects.

They are all intertwined because that's the way reality is. You cannot separate out the technology per se, and instead must consider it within the milieu of what is being invented and innovated, and do so with a mindset towards the contemporary mores and culture that shape what we are doing and what we hope to do.

WHY THIS BOOK

I wrote this book to try and bring to the public view many aspects about self-driving cars that nobody seems to be discussing.

For business leaders that are either involved in making self-driving cars or that are going to leverage self-driving cars, I hope that this book will enlighten you as to the risks involved and ways in which you should be strategizing about how to deal with those risks.

For entrepreneurs, startups and other businesses that want to enter into the self-driving car market that is emerging, I hope this book sparks your interest in doing so, and provides some sense of what might be prudent to pursue.

For researchers that study self-driving cars, I hope this book spurs your interest in the risks and safety issues of self-driving cars, and also nudges you toward conducting research on those aspects.

For students in computer science or related disciplines, I hope this book will provide you with interesting and new ideas and material, for which you might conduct research or provide some career direction insights for you.

For AI companies and high-tech companies pursuing self-driving cars, this book will hopefully broaden your view beyond just the mere coding and development needed to make self-driving cars.

For all readers, I hope that you will find the material in this book to be stimulating. Some of it will be repetitive of things you already know. But I am pretty sure that you'll also find various eureka moments whereby you'll discover a new technique or approach that you had not earlier thought of. I am also betting that there will be material that forces you to rethink some of your current practices.

I am not saying you will suddenly have an epiphany and change what you are doing. I do think though that you will reconsider or perhaps revisit what you are doing.

For anyone choosing to use this book for teaching purposes, please take a look at my suggestions for doing so, as described in the Appendix. I have found the material handy in courses that I have taught, and likewise other faculty have told me that they have found the material handy, in some cases as extended readings and in other instances as a core part of their course (depending on the nature of the class).

In my writing for this book, I have tried carefully to blend both the practitioner and the academic styles of writing. It is not as dense as is typical academic journal writing, but at the same time offers depth by going into the nuances and trade-offs of various practices.

The word "deep" is in vogue today, meaning getting deeply into a subject or topic, and so is the word "unpack" which means to tease out the underlying aspects of a subject or topic. I have sought to offer material that addresses an issue or topic by going relatively deeply into it and make sure that it is well unpacked.

Finally, in any book about AI, it is difficult to use our everyday words without having some of them be misinterpreted. Specifically, it is easy to anthropomorphize AI. When I say that an AI system "knows" something, I do not want you to construe that the AI system has sentience and "knows" in the same way that humans do. They aren't that way, as yet. I have tried to use quotes around such words from time-to-time to emphasize that the words I am using should not be misinterpreted to ascribe true human intelligence to the AI systems that we know of today. If I used quotes around all such words, the book would be very difficult to read, and so I am doing so judiciously. Please keep that in mind as you read the material, thanks.

COMPANION BOOKS

If you find this material of interest, you might want to also see my other books on self-driving cars, entitled:

1. **"Introduction to Driverless Self-Driving Cars"** by Dr. Lance Eliot

2. **"Innovation and Thought Leadership on Self-Driving Driverless Cars"** by Dr. Lance Eliot

3. **"Advances in AI and Autonomous Vehicles: Cybernetic Self-Driving Cars"** by Dr. Lance Eliot

4. ***"Self-Driving Cars: The Mother of All AI Projects"*** by Dr. Lance Eliot

5. **"New Advances in AI Autonomous Driverless Self-Driving Cars"** by Dr. Lance Eliot

6. **"Autonomous Vehicle Driverless Self-Driving Cars and Artificial Intelligence"** by Dr. Lance Eliot and Michael B. Eliot

7. **"Transformative Artificial Intelligence Driverless Self-Driving Cars"** by Dr. Lance Eliot

8. **"Disruptive Artificial Intelligence and Driverless Self-Driving Cars"** by Dr. Lance Eliot

9. "State-of-the-Art AI Driverless Self-Driving Cars" by Dr. Lance Eliot

10. **"Top Trends in AI Self-Driving Cars"** by Dr. Lance Eliot

11. **"AI Innovations and Self-Driving Cars"** by Dr. Lance Eliot

12. **"Crucial Advances for AI Driverless Cars"** by Dr. Lance Eliot

13. **"Sociotechnical Insights and AI Driverless Cars"** by Dr. Lance Eliot.

14. **"Pioneering Advances for AI Driverless Cars"** by Dr. Lance Eliot

15. **"Leading Edge Trends for AI Driverless Cars"** by Dr. Lance Eliot

All of the above books are available on Amazon and at other major global booksellers.

CHAPTER 1

ELIOT FRAMEWORK FOR AI SELF-DRIVING CARS

CHAPTER 1

ELIOT FRAMEWORK FOR AI SELF-DRIVING CARS

This chapter is a core foundational aspect for understanding AI self-driving cars and I have used this same chapter in several of my other books to introduce the reader to essential elements of this field. Once you've read this chapter, you'll be prepared to read the rest of the material since the foundational essence of the components of autonomous AI driverless self-driving cars will have been established for you.

When I give presentations about self-driving cars and teach classes on the topic, I have found it helpful to provide a framework around which the various key elements of self-driving cars can be understood and organized (see diagram at the end of this chapter). The framework needs to be simple enough to convey the overarching elements, but at the same time not so simple that it belies the true complexity of self-driving cars. As such, I am going to describe the framework here and try to offer in a thousand words (or more!) what the framework diagram itself intends to portray.

The core elements on the diagram are numbered for ease of reference. The numbering does not suggest any kind of prioritization of the elements. Each element is crucial. Each element has a purpose, and otherwise would not be included in the framework. For some self-driving cars, a particular element might be more important or somehow distinguished in comparison to other self-driving cars.

17

You could even use the framework to rate a particular self-driving car, doing so by gauging how well it performs in each of the elements of the framework. I will describe each of the elements, one at a time. After doing so, I'll discuss aspects that illustrate how the elements interact and perform during the overall effort of a self-driving car.

At the Cybernetic Self-Driving Car Institute, we use the framework to keep track of what we are working on, and how we are developing software that fills in what is needed to achieve Level 5 self-driving cars.

D-01: Sensor Capture

Let's start with the one element that often gets the most attention in the press about self-driving cars, namely, the sensory devices for a self-driving car.

On the framework, the box labeled as D-01 indicates "Sensor Capture" and refers to the processes of the self-driving car that involve collecting data from the myriad of sensors that are used for a self-driving car. The types of devices typically involved are listed, such as the use of mono cameras, stereo cameras, LIDAR devices, radar systems, ultrasonic devices, GPS, IMU, and so on.

These devices are tasked with obtaining data about the status of the self-driving car and the world around it. Some of the devices are continually providing updates, while others of the devices await an indication by the self-driving car that the device is supposed to collect data. The data might be first transformed in some fashion by the device itself, or it might instead be fed directly into the sensor capture as raw data. At that point, it might be up to the sensor capture processes to do transformations on the data. This all varies depending upon the nature of the devices being used and how the devices were designed and developed.

D-02: Sensor Fusion

Imagine that your eyeballs receive visual images, your nose receives odors, your ears receive sounds, and in essence each of your distinct sensory devices is getting some form of input. The input befits the nature of the device. Likewise, for a self-driving car, the cameras provide visual images, the radar returns radar reflections, and so on.

Each device provides the data as befits what the device does.

At some point, using the analogy to humans, you need to merge together what your eyes see, what your nose smells, what your ears hear, and piece it all together into a larger sense of what the world is all about and what is happening around you. Sensor fusion is the action of taking the singular aspects from each of the devices and putting them together into a larger puzzle.

Sensor fusion is a tough task. There are some devices that might not be working at the time of the sensor capture. Or, there might some devices that are unable to report well what they have detected. Again, using a human analogy, suppose you are in a dark room and so your eyes cannot see much. At that point, you might need to rely more so on your ears and what you hear. The same is true for a self-driving car. If the cameras are obscured due to snow and sleet, it might be that the radar can provide a greater indication of what the external conditions consist of.

In the case of a self-driving car, there can be a plethora of such sensory devices. Each is reporting what it can. Each might have its difficulties. Each might have its limitations, such as how far ahead it can detect an object. All of these limitations need to be considered during the sensor fusion task.

D-03: Virtual World Model

For humans, we presumably keep in our minds a model of the world around us when we are driving a car. In your mind, you know that the car is going at say 60 miles per hour and that you are on a freeway. You have a model in your mind that your car is surrounded by other cars, and that there are lanes to the freeway. Your model is not only based on what you can see, hear, etc., but also what you know about the nature of the world. You know that at any moment that car ahead of you can smash on its brakes, or the car behind you can ram into your car, or that the truck in the next lane might swerve into your lane.

The AI of the self-driving car needs to have a virtual world model, which it then keeps updated with whatever it is receiving from the sensor fusion, which received its input from the sensor capture and the sensory devices.

D-04: System Action Plan

By having a virtual world model, the AI of the self-driving car is able to keep track of where the car is and what is happening around the car. In addition, the AI needs to determine what to do next. Should the self-driving car hit its brakes? Should the self-driving car stay in its lane or swerve into the lane to the left? Should the self-driving car accelerate or slow down?

A system action plan needs to be prepared by the AI of the self-driving car. The action plan specifies what actions should be taken. The actions need to pertain to the status of the virtual world model. Plus, the actions need to be realizable.

This realizability means that the AI cannot just assert that the self-driving car should suddenly sprout wings and fly. Instead, the AI must be bound by whatever the self-driving car can actually do, such as coming to a halt in a distance of X feet at a speed of Y miles per hour, rather than perhaps asserting that the self-driving car come to a halt in 0 feet as though it could instantaneously come to a stop while it is in motion.

D-05: Controls Activation

The system action plan is implemented by activating the controls of the car to act according to what the plan stipulates. This might mean that the accelerator control is commanded to increase the speed of the car. Or, the steering control is commanded to turn the steering wheel 30 degrees to the left or right.

One question arises as to whether or not the controls respond as they are commanded to do. In other words, suppose the AI has commanded the accelerator to increase, but for some reason it does not do so. Or, maybe it tries to do so, but the speed of the car does not increase. The controls activation feeds back into the virtual world model, and simultaneously the virtual world model is getting updated from the sensors, the sensor capture, and the sensor fusion. This allows the AI to ascertain what has taken place as a result of the controls being commanded to take some kind of action.

By the way, please keep in mind that though the diagram seems to have a linear progression to it, the reality is that these are all aspects of the self-driving car that are happening in parallel and simultaneously. The sensors are capturing data, meanwhile the sensor fusion is taking place, meanwhile the virtual model is being updated, meanwhile the system action plan is being formulated and reformulated, meanwhile the controls are being activated.

This is the same as a human being that is driving a car. They are eyeballing the road, meanwhile they are fusing in their mind the sights, sounds, etc., meanwhile their mind is updating their model of the world around them, meanwhile they are formulating an action plan of what to do, and meanwhile they are pushing their foot onto the pedals and steering the car. In the normal course of driving a car, you are doing all of these at once. I mention this so that when you look at the diagram, you will think of the boxes as processes that are all happening at the same time, and not as though only one happens and then the next.

They are shown diagrammatically in a simplistic manner to help comprehend what is taking place. You though should also realize that they are working in parallel and simultaneous with each other. This is a tough aspect in that the inter-element communications involve latency and other aspects that must be taken into account. There can be delays in one element updating and then sharing its latest status with other elements.

D-06: Automobile & CAN

Contemporary cars use various automotive electronics and a Controller Area Network (CAN) to serve as the components that underlie the driving aspects of a car. There are Electronic Control Units (ECU's) which control subsystems of the car, such as the engine, the brakes, the doors, the windows, and so on.

The elements D-01, D-02, D-03, D-04, D-05 are layered on top of the D-06, and must be aware of the nature of what the D-06 is able to do and not do.

D-07: In-Car Commands

Humans are going to be occupants in self-driving cars. In a Level 5 self-driving car, there must be some form of communication that takes place between the humans and the self-driving car. For example, I go into a self-driving car and tell it that I want to be driven over to Disneyland, and along the way I want to stop at In-and-Out Burger. The self-driving car now parses what I've said and tries to then establish a means to carry out my wishes.

In-car commands can happen at any time during a driving journey. Though my example was about an in-car command when I first got into my self-driving car, it could be that while the self-driving car is carrying out the journey that I change my mind. Perhaps after getting stuck in traffic, I tell the self-driving car to forget about getting the burgers and just head straight over to the theme park. The self-driving car needs to be alert to in-car commands throughout the journey.

D-08: VX2 Communications

We will ultimately have self-driving cars communicating with each other, doing so via V2V (Vehicle-to-Vehicle) communications. We will also have self-driving cars that communicate with the roadways and other aspects of the transportation infrastructure, doing so via V2I (Vehicle-to-Infrastructure).

The variety of ways in which a self-driving car will be communicating with other cars and infrastructure is being called V2X, whereby the letter X means whatever else we identify as something that a car should or would want to communicate with. The V2X communications will be taking place simultaneous with everything else on the diagram, and those other elements will need to incorporate whatever it gleans from those V2X communications.

D-09: Deep Learning

The use of Deep Learning permeates all other aspects of the self-driving car. The AI of the self-driving car will be using deep learning to do a better job at the systems action plan, and at the controls activation, and at the sensor fusion, and so on.

Currently, the use of artificial neural networks is the most prevalent form of deep learning. Based on large swaths of data, the neural networks attempt to "learn" from the data and therefore direct the efforts of the self-driving car accordingly.

D-10: Tactical AI

Tactical AI is the element of dealing with the moment-to-moment driving of the self-driving car. Is the self-driving car staying in its lane of the freeway? Is the car responding appropriately to the controls commands? Are the sensory devices working?

For human drivers, the tactical equivalent can be seen when you watch a novice driver such as a teenager that is first driving. They are focused on the mechanics of the driving task, keeping their eye on the road while also trying to properly control the car.

D-11: Strategic AI

The Strategic AI aspects of a self-driving car are dealing with the larger picture of what the self-driving car is trying to do. If I had asked that the self-driving car take me to Disneyland, there is an overall journey map that needs to be kept and maintained.

There is an interaction between the Strategic AI and the Tactical AI. The Strategic AI is wanting to keep on the mission of the driving, while the Tactical AI is focused on the particulars underway in the driving effort. If the Tactical AI seems to wander away from the overarching mission, the Strategic AI wants to see why and get things back on track. If the Tactical AI realizes that there is something amiss on the self-driving car, it needs to alert the Strategic AI accordingly and have an adjustment to the overarching mission that is underway.

D-12: Self-Aware AI

Very few of the self-driving cars being developed are including a Self-Aware AI element, which we at the Cybernetic Self-Driving Car Institute believe is crucial to Level 5 self-driving cars.

The Self-Aware AI element is intended to watch over itself, in the sense that the AI is making sure that the AI is working as intended. Suppose you had a human driving a car, and they were starting to drive erratically. Hopefully, their own self-awareness would make them realize they themselves are driving poorly, such as perhaps starting to fall asleep after having been driving for hours on end. If you had a passenger in the car, they might be able to alert the driver if the driver is starting to do something amiss. This is exactly what the Self-Aware

AI element tries to do, it becomes the overseer of the AI, and tries to detect when the AI has become faulty or confused, and then find ways to overcome the issue.

D-13: Economic

The economic aspects of a self-driving car are not per se a technology aspect of a self-driving car, but the economics do indeed impact the nature of a self-driving car. For example, the cost of outfitting a self-driving car with every kind of possible sensory device is prohibitive, and so choices need to be made about which devices are used. And, for those sensory devices chosen, whether they would have a full set of features or a more limited set of features.

We are going to have self-driving cars that are at the low-end of a consumer cost point, and others at the high-end of a consumer cost point. You cannot expect that the self-driving car at the low-end is going to be as robust as the one at the high-end. I realize that many of the self-driving car pundits are acting as though all self-driving cars will be the same, but they won't be. Just like anything else, we are going to have self-driving cars that have a range of capabilities. Some will be better than others. Some will be safer than others. This is the way of the real-world, and so we need to be thinking about the economics aspects when considering the nature of self-driving cars.

D-14: Societal

This component encompasses the societal aspects of AI which also impacts the technology of self-driving cars. For example, the famous Trolley Problem involves what choices should a self-driving car make when faced with life-and-death matters. If the self-driving car is about to either hit a child standing in the roadway, or instead ram into a tree at the side of the road and possibly kill the humans in the self-driving car, which choice should be made?

We need to keep in mind the societal aspects will underlie the AI of the self-driving car. Whether we are aware of it explicitly or not, the AI will have embedded into it various societal assumptions.

D-15: Innovation

I included the notion of innovation into the framework because we can anticipate that whatever a self-driving car consists of, it will continue to be innovated over time. The self-driving cars coming out in the next several years will undoubtedly be different and less innovative than the versions that come out in ten years hence, and so on.

Framework Overall

For those of you that want to learn about self-driving cars, you can potentially pick a particular element and become specialized in that aspect. Some engineers are focusing on the sensory devices. Some engineers focus on the controls activation. And so on. There are specialties in each of the elements.

Researchers are likewise specializing in various aspects. For example, there are researchers that are using Deep Learning to see how best it can be used for sensor fusion. There are other researchers that are using Deep Learning to derive good System Action Plans. Some are studying how to develop AI for the Strategic aspects of the driving task, while others are focused on the Tactical aspects.

A well-prepared all-around software developer that is involved in self-driving cars should be familiar with all of the elements, at least to the degree that they know what each element does. This is important since whatever piece of the pie that the software developer works on, they need to be knowledgeable about what the other elements are doing.

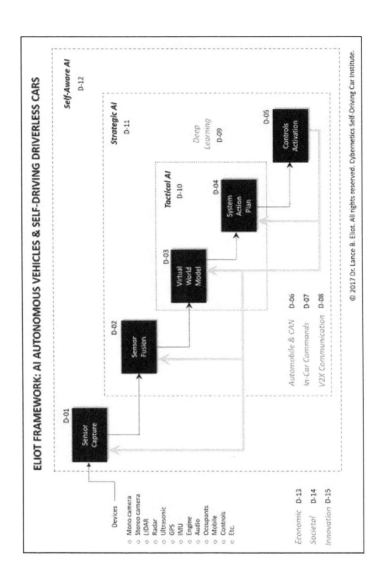

CHAPTER 2

PRANKING AND AI SELF-DRIVING CARS

CHAPTER 2

PRANKING AND
AI SELF-DRIVING CARS

When you do a prank on someone, it hopefully is done in jest and with no particular adverse consequences. You've likely seen the many YouTube videos of people pulling pranks on other people. Sometimes, these are innocent pranks and seemingly other than the surprise to the person being pranked, there isn't any lasting negative impacts. There are though pranks that go-over-the-line, so to speak, and at times cause harm to the target of the prank and possibly to others too.

Some would say that pranks are fun, interesting, and not a big deal. Even those that pull pranks would likely reluctantly admit that you can take things too far. A good friend of mine got hurt when someone with them at a bar opted to suddenly pull their chair away from the table when they had gotten up, and the friend upon trying to sit back down, unknowingly and shockingly went all the way to the floor. The impact to the floor hurt their back, neck, and nearly caused a head concussion. My friend went to the local emergency room for a quick check-up. A seemingly "fun" joke that was meant to be harmless, turned out to have serious consequences.

Of course, pranks can be purposely designed to be foul. Some years ago, when I was a professor, a colleague was upset with someone and opted to "prank them" by messing with a research project the person had labored on for several months. The colleague went into the lab where the experiment had been gradually evolving and made some changes that were unbeknownst to the principle researcher.

The principle researcher later found that their results seemed quite odd, and eventually traced it to someone having intervened in the experiment. This set her back many months on the work. This was not an accidental kind of prank result, but one done by determination. The person that did the prank tried to pretend that they had no idea that doing the prank would cause such difficulty. Most everyone didn't buy into his rather hollow attempt to act naïve about the situation.

Let's shift attention from the notion of pranks to something similar to a prank, but we'll recast it in different terms.

Sometimes in a sport like basketball or football, you might use a feint or dodge to try and fool your opponent and gain a competitive advantage over them. While dribbling a basketball, you might move your body to the right as though you are going to head in that direction, and then suddenly swerve instead to your left. This feint or "fake" move can be instrumental to how you play the sport. It isn't something that you do just on rare occasion, but instead it's an ongoing tactic or even strategy for playing the game.

When you consider the sport of fencing, feints are the lifeblood of the competition. You want your opponent to think you are going to lunge at them, but you don't actually do so. Or, you want them to think you are not going to lunge at them, but you do so. Typically, a so-called feint attack consists of making the appearance of an attack to provoke a response from the other fencer. If they fall for the trap, you've then got them in a posture wherein you can potentially undertake a true attack.

There's also the feint retreat, which usually consists of actively engaging your opponent and then make a fast retreat, even though they might think you are coming on strong toward them and therefore have reacted accordingly. When you watch a fencing match, it is a fast paced and consists of a dizzying series of rapid feints. In a sport like basketball or football, feints tend to occur over a period of many seconds of time, while in fencing it can be occurring in split seconds of time. Each fencer is trying to do feints to the other, and each is trying to detect the feints and react in a manner best suited to counteract the feint of the other.

What does this have to do with AI self-driving cars?

At the Cybernetic AI Self-Driving Car Institute, we are developing AI systems for self-driving cars. One of the concerns currently about AI self-driving cars is that some people are trying prank them.

Allow me to elaborate.

The AI of today's self-driving cars is still quite crude in comparison to where we all hope to be down-the-road. Generally, you can consider the AI to be a very timid driver. It would be as though you had a novice teenager that's first learning to drive. You've probably seen teenage drivers that go very slowly, take turns with great caution, ride their brakes, come to full and lengthy stops at stop signs, and so on. In some sense, the AI for self-driving cars is currently performing in a like manner.

You need to be aware that there are various levels of AI self-driving cars. The topmost level is referred to as Level 5. A Level 5 self-driving car is one that is supposed to be able to drive the car without any human driver needed. Thus, the AI needs to be able to drive the car as though it was as proficient as a human driver. This is not easy to do. I've mentioned many times that to have AI that's good enough to be like a proficient human driver is nearly akin to achieving a moonshot.

For self-driving cars less than a Level 5, it is assumed and required that a human driver be present. Furthermore, the human driver is considered responsible for the driving task, in spite of the aspect that the driving is being co-shared by the human driver and the AI system. I've said many times that this notion of a co-shared driving effort is problematic and we're going to have lots of deadly consequences. In any case, for the purposes of this pranking topic, I'm going to focus on the Level 5 self-driving car, though in many respects my comments are applicable to the less than Level 5 self-driving cars too.

So, we've got AI right now that drives a Level 5 self-driving car in the simplest of ways, being at times akin to a teenage driver (though, don't over ascribe that analogy; the AI is not at all "thinking" and thus not similar to a human mind, even that of a teenager!). The AI is driving the self-driving car and taking lots of precautions. This makes sense in that the auto makers and tech firms don't want an AI self-driving car to be driving in a manner that could add risk to having an incident occur. The media is poised to clamor about self-driving car incidents, plus of course the auto maker and tech firm doesn't intentionally want to have human injuries or deaths (though, their actions via their AI self-driving cars might lead to such results).

You've got a kind of grand convergence in that some people have figured out how timid these AI self-driving cars are, and of those people, there are some that have opted to take advantage of the circumstances. As I'll emphasize in a moment, more and more people are going to similarly opt to "prank" AI self-driving cars.

When AI self-driving cars first started appearing, it was considered a novelty and most people kept clear of an AI self-driving car. They did so because they were surprised to even encounter one. It was like suddenly seeing an aardvark, which you'd heard exist, but you'd not seen one with your own eyes. You would give such a creature a wide berth, wanting to see what it does and how it does things. This was the "amazement" phase of people reacting to AI self-driving cars.

In addition, most of the time, the AI self-driving cars were being tried out on public roads in relatively high-tech areas. Places like Sunnyvale, California and Palo Alto. These are geographical areas that are dominated by tech firms and tech employees. As a tech person, if you saw an AI self-driving car, you were somewhat in the "amazement" category, but perhaps more so in the "this is someone else's experiment and I respect their efforts" category. You weren't necessarily in awe, but more so curious and also figured that you'd prefer that people don't mess with your tech creations, so you should do the same about their tech creations.

One of the early on stories about how the AI reacts in a timid manner consisted of the now famous four-way stop tale. It is said that an AI self-driving car would come to a four-way stop, and do what's expected, namely come to a full and complete stop. Do humans also come to a full and complete stop? Unless you live in some place that consists of rigorously law-abiding human drivers, I dare say that many people do a rolling stop. They come up to the stop sign and if it looks presumably safe to do so, they continue rolling forward and into the intersection.

In theory, we are all supposed to come to a complete stop and then judge as to which car should proceed if more than one car has now stopped at the four-way stop. I'm sure you've had situations wherein you arrived at the stop sign just a second or two before another car, and yet that other human driver decided to move ahead, even though they should have deferred to you. It can be exasperating and quite irritating. There are some human drivers that think other human drivers are like sheep, and if they are a wolf they will be happy to dominate over the sheep.

Well, the AI self-driving car detected that other cars were coming up to or at the stop sign on the other sides of the four-way stop. The AI then calculated that it should identify what those other cars are going to do. If a human inadvertently misreads a stop sign and maybe doesn't even realize it is there, and therefore barrels into an intersection, you would certainly want to have the AI self-driving car not mistakenly enter into the intersection and get into an untoward incident with that ditzy human driver. Crash, boom.

But, suppose those human drivers weren't necessarily ditzy and were just driving as humans do. They came up to the stop sign and did a traditional rolling stop. The AI of the self-driving car would likely interpret the rolling stop as an indicator that the other car is not going to keep the intersection clear. The right choice then would be for the AI to keep the self-driving car at the stop sign, waiting until the coast is clear.

Suppose though that human driven cars, one after another, all did the same rolling stop. The AI, being timid or cautious, allegedly sat there, waiting patiently for its turn. I think we can all envision a teenage driver doing something similar. The teenage driver might not want to assert themselves over the more seasoned drivers. The teenage driver probably would figure that waiting was better than taking a chance on getting rammed in the middle of the intersection. In a manner of consideration, the AI was doing something similar.

Was it coincidental that the other cars, the human driver cars, proceeded each to do a rolling stop? It could be. But, it could also be that they noticed that the other car waiting at the stop sign was an AI self-driving car. These clever humans might have wondered whether the AI was going to move forward or not. If it appeared that the self-driving car was sitting still, it would be like realizing that a teenage driver has frozen at the wheel and won't take action. You might as well then just proceed. No need to wait for the teenage driver to realize they can go. This same logic likely was used by some of the human drivers as to not allowing the AI per se to proceed.

Is this a prank then by those human drivers upon an AI self-driving car?

I suppose you might argue with the use of the word "prank" in this case. Were those humans trying to pull away the seat of someone before they sat down? Were these humans messing with someone's experiment as a means to get revenge? In one sense, you could argue that they were pranking the AI self-driving car, and doing so to gain an advantage over the AI self-driving car (didn't want to wait at a four-way stop). You could also argue that it wasn't a prank per se, but more like a maneuver to keep traffic flowing (in their minds they might have perceived this), and perhaps it is like a feint in a sport.

Imagine if the human driver coming up to the four-way stop tried to do a rolling stop, but meanwhile another human driven car did the same thing. You'd likely end-up with a game of chicken. Each would challenge the other. If you dare to move forward, I will too. The other driver is thinking the same.

I've seen this actually happen. At one point, as ridiculous as it might seem, I saw two cars that were in the middle of an intersection, each crawling forward, each unwilling to give up territory for the other car. It's crazy too because they were holding up other traffic and making things go slowly even for their own progress. What idiots! People at times get into a possessive mode when behind the wheel of a car. They are willing to play games of chicken, in spite of the rather apparent dangers of doing so with multi-ton cars that can harm or kill people.

The four-way stop example showcases the situation of an AI self-driving car and its relationship to human driven cars. There's also the circumstances of a pedestrian messing around with an AI self-driving car.

Depending upon where you live in the world, you've probably seen pedestrians that try to mess with human drivers of conventional cars. In New York, it seems an essential part of life to stare down human drivers when you are crossing the street, especially when jaywalking. There are some New Yorkers that seem to think that the mere act of making eye contact with a human driver will promote a safe journey across a street. It's as though your eyes are laser beams or something like that. This is also why many New York drivers won't make eye contact with a pedestrian, since it's a means of pretending the pedestrian doesn't exist. You can just blindly proceed, and the pedestrian better stay out of the way.

There is no ready means to do a traditional stare down with an AI self-driving car. Presumably, a pedestrian would then be mindful to be less risky when trying to negotiate the crossing of a street. They can no longer make the eye contact that says don't you dare drive there and get in my pedestrian way. Instead, the AI self-driving car is going to be possibly do whatever it darned well pleases to do.

I'd gauge that most pedestrians right now are willing to give an AI self-driving car a wide berth, but this is only if they even realize it is an AI self-driving car. There are many AI self-driving cars that are easily recognizable because they have a conehead shape on the top of the self-driving car (usually containing the LIDAR sensor). Once again fitting into the "amazement" category, pedestrians are in awe to see one drive past them. Give it room, is the thought most people likely have.

But, if you see them all the time and instantly recognize them, the awe factor is gone. Furthermore, if they are traveling slowly and acting in a timid matter, well, you've got better things to do than wait around for some stupid AI self-driving car to makes its way down the street. It could also be that you don't even realize it is an AI self-driving car, either because it doesn't have that look of an AI self-driving car, or you aren't paying attention to the traffic and just opt to do what pedestrians often do, namely jaywalk.

In a manner similar to the four-way stop, you can often get an AI self-driving car to halt or change its course, doing so by some simple trickery. The AI is likely trying to detect pedestrians that appear to be a "threat" to the driving task. If you are standing on the sidewalk and a few feet from the curb, and you are standing still, you would be likely marked as a low threat or non-threat. If you instead were at the curb, your threat level increases. If you are in-motion and going in the direction of the street and where the AI self-driving car is headed, your threat risk increases further.

Knowing this, you can potentially fool the AI into assuming that you are going to jaywalk. Given the timid nature of the AI, it will likely then calculate that it might be safer to come to a stop and let you do so, or maybe swerve to let you do so. If you have one pedestrian try this, and it works to halt the AI self-driving car, and if there are more pedestrians nearby that witness this, they too will likely opt to play the same trick. Similar again to the four-way stop, you might have person after person, each of them making motions to get into the street, and the AI opting to just keep waiting until those pesky pedestrians are no longer consider a threat to proceeding.

You don't need an AI self-driving car to see this same kind of phenomena occurring. Drive to any downtown area that is filled with pedestrians. If those pedestrians' sense that you are a sheep, they will take advantage of the situation. Many pedestrians use age as a factor in ascertaining whether to assert their pedestrian rights, such as if they see a teenage driver or a senior citizen driver. Some will gauge the situation by the type of car or how the car is moving down the street. And so on.

As we increasingly have more AI self-driving cars on our roadways, I'll predict that the "amazement" category will fade and instead will be replaced with the "prank" an AI self-driving car mindset.

Some AI developers that are working on AI self-driving cars are dumbfounded when I make such a prediction. They believe fervently in the great value to society that AI self-driving cars will bring. They cannot fathom why people would mess around with this. Don't those pedestrians realize that they are potentially undermining the future of mankind?

Why would people mess around with AI self-driving cars in this "prank" kind of way? I have lots of reasons why people would do so.

Here's some of the likely reasons:

·   Why did the chicken cross the road, in order to get to the other side. If humans, whether as drivers or pedestrians, perceive that an AI self-driving car is essentially in their way, some of those humans are going to find a means to keep it from getting in their way. These humans will simply outmaneuver the AI self-driving car, as such, one of the easiest means will be to do a feint and the AI self-driving car will do the rest for the human.

- Humans at times like to show that they are as smart or even smarter than automation. What can be more ego boosting than to outwit a seemingly supreme AI system that's driving a car?

- Some humans are frankly show-offs. Watch me, a pedestrian says to anyone nearby, as I trick a human driver into thinking I'm going to jump into the street and that driver will freak out. Equally treasured if it's an AI system that gets freaked out.

- Humans love sports. They event new sports all the time. Remember planking? Well, one brand new sport will be pranking an AI self-driving car. Imagine the YouTube videos and the number of views for the most outlandish pranks that successfully confounded an AI self-driving car.

- They say that curiosity killed the cat. Don't know about that. A human though is likely to be curious about AI self-driving cars and what makes them tick. Wouldn't you be tempted to as a pedestrian wave your arms in the air and see if it causes an AI self-driving car to react? Of course, you would.

- There are some that believe AI is a potential doomsday path for society. In that case, you'd want to provide tangible examples of how AI can get things goofed-up. Making an AI self-driving car do something that we would not expect a human driven car to do, or that shows how much less capable the AI is than a human, it's a likely gold star for anyone aiming to take down AI.

- There could be some people that will ponder whether they might somehow help AI self-driving cars by purposely trying to prank them. If you come up behind your friend and say boo, the next time someone else does it, they'll hopefully be better prepared. Some people will assume that if they prank an AI self-driving car, it will learn from it, and then no longer be so gullible. They might be right, or they might be mistaken to believe that the AI will get anything out of it (this depends on how the AI developers developed the AI for the self-driving car).

There you have it, a plethora of reasons that people will be tempted to prank an AI self-driving car. I can come up with more reasons, but I think you get the idea that we are heading toward a situation wherein a lot of people will be motivated to undertake such pranks.

What's going to stop these pranksters?

Some auto makers and tech firms, and especially some AI developers, believe that we should go the root of the problem. What is that root? In their minds, it's the pesky and bothersome human that's the problem.

As such, such advocates say that we should enact laws that will prevent humans from pranking AI self-driving cars.

In this view, if you have tough enough penalties, whether monetary fines or jail time, it will make pranksters think twice and stop their dastardly ways. I don't want to seem unsympathetic to this notion, but can you imagine two people in prison, one says to the other that they committed armed robbery, and the other one says that he waved his arms at an AI self-driving car and got busted for it.

Overall, it's not clear that a regulatory means of solving the problem will be much help in the matter. I'm sure that law abiding people will certainly abide by such a new law. Lawbreakers would seem less likely, unless there's a magical way to readily catch them at their crime and prosecute them for it. The AI developers would say that it's easy to capture that the person did a prank, since the AI self-driving car will undoubtedly record video and other sensory data that could presumably be used to support the assertion that the human pulled a prank on the AI self-driving car.

If we go down that rabbit hole, how exactly are we to ascertain that someone was carrying out a prank? Maybe the person was waving their arms or making their way into the street, and they had no idea an AI self-driving car was there. Also, are we going to outlaw the prankster doing the same thing to a human driver? If not, could the prankster claim they were making the motions toward a human driver and not the AI? Or, they though the AI self-driving car was being driven by a human and couldn't see into the car well enough to see if there was a human driver there or not.

I'd say that the legal approach would be an untenable morass.

There are some though that counter-argue that when trains first became popular, people eventually figured out to not prank trains. It was presumably easy for someone to stand in the train tracks and possibly get an entire train to come to a halt. But, this supposedly never took root. Some say there are laws against it, depending upon which geographical area you are in. Certainly, one could also say that there are more general laws that could apply in terms of endangering others and yourself.

Culturally, we could try to blast those that conduct pranks. Make them outcasts of society. This might potentially have some impact on the pranksters. If you go along with the idea that AI self-driving cars are overall a boon for society, it's conceivable that there could become a cultural momentum towards wanting to "help" the beleaguered AI and try to castigate the human pranksters that go the opposite direction by trying to confound the AI.

Some say that we should have a consumer education campaign to make people aware of the limitations of AI self-driving cars. Perhaps the government could sponsor such a campaign, maybe even making it mandatory viewing by government workers. It could be added into school programs. Businesses maybe would be incentivized to educate their employees about fooling around with pranking of AI self-driving cars.

Some are a bit more morbid and suggest that once a few people are injured by having pranked an AI self-driving, and once some people are killed, it will cause people generally to realize that doing a prank on an AI self-driving car has some really bad consequences. People will realize that it makes no sense to try and fool AI self-driving cars since it can cause lives to be lost.

These and similar arguments are all predicated on the same overarching theme, namely that the AI is the AI, and that the thing that needs to be changed is humans and human behavior.

I'd be willing to wager a bet that people will not be willing to accept an AI system that can be so readily pranked. If it comes down to whether to enact laws to stop people from pranking, or culturally trying to stop them from pranking, or providing consumer education, in the end it's more likely that there will be a clamor for better AI. Indeed, there is a greater chance of people saying keep the AI off-the-road, rather than having a willingness to change the behavior of people due to AI that can't cope with pranksters.

I know that this disappoints many of those AI developers that are prone to pointing the finger at the humans, and in their view it's better, easier, faster to change human behavior. I would suggest that we ought to be looking instead at the AI and not delude ourselves into believing that mediocre AI will carry the day and force society to adjust to it.

I realize there are some that contend that people won't somehow figure out that they can prank AI self-driving cars. Maybe only a few people here or there will do so, but it won't be a mainstream activity.

I'd like to suggest we burst that bubble. I assure you that once AI self-driving cars start becoming prevalent, people will use social media to share readily all the ways to trick, fool, deceive, or prank an AI self-driving car. Word will spread like wildfire.

You know how some software systems have hidden Easter eggs? In a manner of speaking, the weaknesses of the AI systems for self-driving cars will be viewed in the same light. People will delight in finding these eggs. Say, did you hear that the AI self-driving car model X will pull over to the curb if you run directly at it while the self-driving car is going less than 5 miles per hour?

This though is also going to create its own havoc. The tips about how to prank an AI self-driving car will include suggestions that aren't even true. People will make them up out-of-the-blue. You'll then have some dolt that will try it on an AI self-driving car, and when the self-driving car nearly hits them, they'll maybe realize they were duped into believing a false prank.

It could be that true prank tips might also no longer work on an AI self-driving car. As mentioned earlier, there is a chance that the Machine Learning (ML) of the AI might catch onto a prank and then be able to avoid falling victim to it again. There's also the OTA (Over

The Air) updating of AI self-driving cars, wherein the auto maker or tech firm can beam into the AI self-driving various updates and patches. If the auto makers or tech firm gets wind of a prank, they might be able to come up with a fix and have it sent to the AI self-driving cars.

This though has its own difficulties. People may not yet realize that the AI self-driving cars are not homogenous and that the nature of the AI systems differs by the auto maker or tech firm. Thus, you might learn of a prank that works on the AI self-driving car brand X, but not on another brand Y. Or, maybe works on brand X model 2, but not on the brand X model 3.

In short, though I am not one to say that a technological problem must always have a technological solution, I'd vote in this case that there should be more attention toward having the AI be good enough that it cannot be readily pranked.

We need to focus on anti-pranking capabilities for AI self-driving cars.

I say this and realize that in so doing that I am laying down a gauntlet for others to help pick-up and run with. We are doing the same.

This is a difficult problem to solve and not one that lends itself to any quick or easy solution. I know that some of you might say that an AI self-driving car needs to shed its tepidness. By being more brazen, it would be able to not only overcome most pranks, it would create a reputation that says don't mess with me, I'm AI that's not be played for a fool.

Here's an example of why that's not so easy to achieve. A pedestrian walks into the middle of the street, right in front of where an AI self-driving car is heading. Let's assume we don't know whether it's a prank. Maybe the pedestrian is drunk. Maybe the pedestrian is looking at their smartphone and is unaware of the approaching car. Or, maybe it is indeed a prank.

What would you have the AI do? If it was a human driver, we'd assume and expect that the human driver will try to stop the car or maneuver to avoid hitting the pedestrian. Is this because the human is timid? Not really. Even the most brazen of human drivers is likely to take evasive action. They might first honk the horn, and maybe shine their headlights, and do anything they can to get the human to get out of the way, but if it comes down to hitting the pedestrian, most human drivers will try to avoid doing so.

Indeed, for just the same reasons, I'm a strong proponent of having AI self-driving cars become more conspicuous in such circumstances. My view is that an AI self-driving car should use the same means that humans do when trying to warn someone or draw attention to their car. Honk the horn. Make a scene. This is something that we're already working on and urge the auto makers and tech firms to do likewise.

Nonetheless, if that human pedestrian wont budge, the car, whether human driven or self-driving, will have to do something to try and avoid the hitting of the pedestrian.

That being said, some humans play such games with other humans, by first estimating whether they believe the human driver will back-down or not. As such, there is some credence to the idea that the AI needs to be more firm about what it is doing. If it is seen as a patsy, admittedly people will rely upon that. This doesn't take us to the extreme posture that the AI needs to therefore hit or run someone down to intentionally prove its mettle.

In the case of the four-way stop situation, I've commented many times that if the other human drivers realized that the AI self-driving car was willing to play the same game of doing a rolling stop, it would cause those human drivers to be less prone to pulling the stunt of the rolling stop to get the AI self-driving car into a bind. I've indicated over and over that AI self-driving cars are going to from time-to-time be "illegal" drivers. I know this makes some go nuts since they are living in a Utopian world whereby no AI self-driving car ever breaks the law, but that's not so easily applied in the real-world of driving.

Some say too that two illegal acts, one by the human driver and one by the AI, does not make a right. I'd agree with that overall point, but also would like to note that there are "small" illegal driving acts happening every day by every human driver. I know its tempting to say that we should hold AI self-driving cars to a higher standard, but this does not comport with the realities of driving in a world of mixed human driving and AI driving. We are not going to have only and exclusively AI self-driving cars on our roadway, and no human driven cars, for a very long time.

There's also the viewpoint that AI self-driving cars can team-up with each other to either avoid pranks or learn from pranks on a shared basis. With the advent of V2V (vehicle-to-vehicle communications), AI self-driving cars will be able to electronically communicate with each other. In the case of a prank, it could be that one self-driving car detects a prankster trying a prank on it, and then the AI shares this with the next self-driving cars coming down that same street. As such, then all of those AI self-driving cars might be ready to contend with the prank.

Unfortunately, there's also another side of that coin. Suppose the AI of a self-driving car inadvertently misleads another AI self-driving car into anticipating a prank when in fact there isn't one coming up. It's a false positive. This could readily occur. The forewarned AI self-driving car has to be savvy enough to determine what action to take, or not to take, not simply by the word shared with it from other AI self-driving car.

If you introduced a slew of teenage drivers into our roadways, doing so all at once, what would happen? Presumably, you'd have tons of timid human drivers that would not take the kinds of shortcuts that more seasoned human drivers have learned over time. Some hope or believe that the AI self-driving cars will do the same. In essence, over time, with the use of Machine Learning and via OTA updates by the AI developers, the AI self-driving cars will get better at more "brazen" driving aspects.

Depending upon the pace at which AI self-driving cars are adopted, some think that maybe the initial small population of AI self-driving cars will take the brunt of the pranking and this will then be overcome by those AI self-driving cars getting us to the next generation of AI self-driving cars. It will be a blip that people at one time pranked the AI self-driving cars in their early days of roadway trials (remember when you could stick out your leg and pretend you were kicking toward an AI self-driving car, and it would honk its horn at you – what a fun prank that was!).

I'd suggest we need to take a more overt approach to this matter and not just hope or assume that the "early day" AI self-driving cars will come through on getting better at dealing with pranks. We need to be building anti-pranking into AI self-driving cars. We need to be boosting the overall driving capabilities of AI self-driving cars to be more human-like. Having AI self-driving cars on our roadways that can too easily fall for a feint attack or a feint retreat, well, those kinds of AI self-driving cars are going to potentially spoil the public's interest and desire in having AI self-driving cars on our roadways. There will always be human pranksters, it's likely in the human DNA. Face reality and let's make sure the "DNA" of AI self-driving cars is anti-prank encoded.

CHAPTER 3

DRIVE-THRUS AND AI SELF-DRIVING CARS

CHAPTER 3

DRIVE-THRUS AND
AI SELF-DRIVING CARS

I used a drive-thru fast food restaurant to get my dinner the other night and became aware that doing so at 6:30 p.m. was not the best time choice. Cars were stacked up like planes at a busy airport. What normally would have taken a few easy minutes to do, including placing my order, paying, and getting my order, turned into so lengthy a wait that I am pretty sure I could have cooked my own meal in the same time period (including the time to purchase the ingredients at the grocery store!).

Anyway, it was my fault too for using the drive-thru at a peak dinner time. Going to a sit-down restaurant would have been even worse of a wait and indeed last week I waited nearly two hours to get a table in a popular downtown Los Angeles eatery. After getting seated that night, it took another twenty minutes to have a waiter take my order. By the time the food arrived, I do believe that I had fallen to the floor from starvation and they had to pump the food into me. Well, maybe that's a bit of an exaggeration.

Let's discuss drive-thru operations.

In the United States, there's an estimated 200,000 or so drive-thru operations (possibly a lot more, depending upon how you are counting). Some statistics claim that Americans do about 6 billion drive-thru "visits" each year. For these kinds of stats, they often count

51

only fast food drive-thru operations, while other counts include our drive-thru efforts at pharmacies to get prescriptions and at banks to use ATM's. The drive-thru is essential to most of the fast food restaurants, including for Starbucks about 40% of their locations have a drive-thru, and in the case of McDonald's it accounts for 70% of their business in the United States.

My experience the other night of having had a long wait time for getting fast food is actually an anomaly. According to fast food drive-thru insiders, the average total time to navigate through the drive-thru and pop out the other side with your food is around 3.5 minutes. That's pretty quick. The streamlined drive-thru fast food restaurants actually aim at a 3-minute average time, well undercutting the 3 ½ minutes norm.

Of course, as a drive-thru operator, you can try to trick the drive-thru times by doing a lousy job in terms of accuracy of the order. If you just jam together a customer order and shove it out the window, not knowing whether your team got the order right or not, you can possibly shave some additional time from the timekeeper. This might be faster since you are pushing your people to move speedily and not do any particular double-checking or have much tender-loving care in the handing of the order. It's a "pure transaction" kind of mindset and the clock is the kingpin. The problem with inaccurate orders is that customers might decide not to come back to your drive-thru ever again, once they get home and discover the botched order, and so the drive-thru will ultimately suffer accordingly.

To try and prevent this kind of sneak around by those manning the drive-thru, most drive-thru owners also track accuracy rates. Generally, the accuracy rate is around 90% for fast food drive-thru operations. This might seem good, since you are getting 9 out of every 10 orders right, but that also means that 10% of the time or around 1 out of every 10 drive-thru orders will be fulfilled inaccurately. That's not something to be proud of. The drive-thru operations are striving for more like a 93-95% accuracy average, though it takes a lot of attention and strident controls to get there.

You might assume that McDonald's was the ground breaker in terms of establishing drive-thru fast food in the United States. Surprise! The fast food approach was first started by a restaurant in Springfield, Missouri in 1947, and then a few years later in 1951 it was Jack In The Box that became the first widespread chain to adopt drive-thru operations. We've become quite a fast food nation since those days. As an aside, though the focus herein is fast food drive-thru, you might find of interest that there are some rather unusual drive-thru businesses beyond fast food, including in Las Vegas you can get married via using a drive-thru (and, I wonder, can you say that you'd like fries with that?).

Why do we seem to so greatly utilize drive-thru fast food restaurants?

It's quite a convenience to do so. You are in your car, driving along, and you get hungry or know that you will soon be hungry. Going to a sit-down restaurant is laborious in that you need to park your car, go into the restaurant, find a place to sit inside the restaurant, you need to order your food and get it brought to your table, and when you are done with the meal there's usually a wait time to get the bill and pay for it. Plus, you then need to exit the restaurant, maybe having cleaned your table before doing so, and you need to get back to your parked car. Exhausting. Time consuming.

Via a drive-thru, you remain in your car, you can expeditiously order and get your food, and then take your food to whatever desired location that you'd like to consume it. Generally, no need to park related to getting the food, or at least no need to drive around trying to find a place to park (I realize that some drive-thru operations will ask you to temporarily park your car while your order is being filled, but they normally have designated parking spots for this purpose, thus no need for you to endlessly search to find a parking spot like doing so at most sit-down restaurants).

So, I think we'd all agree that the drive-thru is a time saver. It also is convenient since it dispenses with the other logistics involved in doing a sit-down.

Some people also like the drive-thru because they can be dressed informally (maybe even in PJ's!), and use a drive-thru, while if they did a sit-down they'd feel obligated to be a bit more properly attired. When my children were young, I admit that the drive-thru was nice because having to get the children out of their car seats was a chore and once inside a restaurant they would not sit still. Please though know that I didn't always choose the drive-thru, and indeed many of the fast food places were quite alluring for a sit down with the children due to the playgrounds that they restaurants cleverly put in place (a great way to give the kids a chance to burn-off energy and have some romping fun).

There have been some backlashes against fast food restaurants, namely that they have too easily made available food that is not nutritious and essentially the food provided is bad for us. There are those that accuse the drive-thru operations as having subliminally led our society to becoming overweight. Sure, it's convenient and a time saver, but maybe also harming us too. It has been like dangling candy in front of a baby. We as a society have fallen "victim" to the ease of drive-thru fast food, and in the end it has produced obesity and weight related health issues for the whole society.

The fast food chains have tried to at times to change the nature of the food offered, attempting to make the food products more nutritious. They have also at times posted indications of the calories and fat content, along with other nutritional information. Some would say that the fast food places have only taken these "corrective" actions when dragged to it via new regulations and not because they appear to genuinely believe it is better for the consumers of the fast food.

I'm not going to address herein the topic of whether fast food is right or wrong, and nor whether the drive-thru was possibly an evil more than a good. Instead, I'd like to focus on the drive-thru as a phenomenon in of itself and consider various aspects about it.

Indeed, you might be wondering, what does this have to do with AI self-driving cars?

At the Cybernetic AI Self-Driving Car Institute, we are developing AI systems for self-driving cars. One interesting aspect of self-driving cars is how they will do when trying to make use of a fast food drive-thru.

When I bring up at my industry presentations the notion of AI self-driving cars being able to navigate through a fast food drive-thru, I sometimes get a groan from people that want to complain about how bad fast food is for us as a society. They then say that it seems like a rotten use of a new-fangled innovation like AI self-driving cars to continue to "poison" ourselves by using fast food drive-thrus.

I've even had some that have insisted that the AI should refuse to use a fast food drive-thru. This would seem to be a means to prevent furtherance of the fast food drive-thru evil bidding. The AI becomes a kind of savior of humans, by not allowing those humans to harm themselves via fast food.

Well, I have one thing to say about this. You must be crazy to think that people are not going to want to continue using fast food drive-thru operations. They are going to want to do so. Furthermore, trying to use the AI as a kind of mother hen, I doubt very much that people will stand for this. They would likely be aghast that the AI refuses to make use of a drive-thru. Using an AI self-driving car to somehow solve a perceived society "problem" of the use of fast food is just not the right kind of tool to be used for that purpose, I assert.

Now, please be aware that I do provide those people with some hope, doing so in the following way. I point out that with their AI self-driving car, they will likely be able to provide various of their own restrictions to where the AI self-driving car can go. For example, since it is likely that people will use their AI self-driving car to take their children to school or to baseball practice after school, the parents could conceivably instruct the AI that the children are not to be allowed to use the AI self-driving car to go to a fast food drive-thru.

In that sense, if people want to selectively choose not to use a fast food drive-thru, they can certainly choose that option. This though is a personal choice. It's not a government mandated choice. It is not up to Big Brother, but instead up to society members to choose what they wish to do. Just as today, when you are driving a car, there's nothing compelling you to use a fast food drive-thru. Similarly, the AI is not presumably going to compel you to use a fast food drive-thru. Plus, you can intentionally instruct the AI to not use a fast food drive-thru. That's of your choosing.

I also point out to those advocating that the AI would somehow be universally pre-programmed to not allow visiting a fast food drive-thru are taking things down a rather slippery slope. What else would you then say that the AI should prevent us from doing? Suppose you believe that shopping malls are bad for us. Would we then pre-program all AI self-driving cars to never go to malls? Suppose you believe that churches are bad – would we then pre-program all AI self-driving cars to never go to churches?

The point is that using the AI to become a controller of human society is something that we'll all need to be very thoughtful about and consider whether this makes sense to do, and how it would be appropriately undertaken, if at all. The irony is that most pundits say that the advent of AI self-driving cars will unleash mobility and we'll become a mobility-as-a-society economy. Kind of ironic to think that this might be used against us, in that the AI also allows potentially for controlling where people can go with their cars.

I'd like to proceed for the moment with the assumption that AI self-driving cars will be used to go to fast food drive-thrus. Let's take a closer look at the practical aspects of how that would occur.

There are some auto makers and tech firms that say that the use of a drive-thru is outside the scope of their current efforts for AI self-driving cars. They perceive that the core capabilities of an AI self-driving car include driving around on our streets and navigating our roads. Sure, it can also navigate a parking lot and park the car. But, the intricacies of a drive-thru are not in their wheelhouse, for now. It's a much lower priority and someday they'll consider providing such a capability.

In that sense, they are suggesting that the navigation of a drive-thru is considered an "edge" problem for AI self-driving cars. An edge problem in the computer field is considered anything at the periphery of whatever you are otherwise trying to solve. I've had AI developers tell me that people should just use sit-down restaurants and not worry about using drive-thru operations, at least for the foreseeable future in terms of the first iterations of AI self-driving cars.

I have a feeling that if you asked the fast food chains whether they care about AI self-driving cars not being able to navigate a drive-thru, you'd get a resounding yes that they do indeed care about whether AI self-driving cars can do so or not. Right now, the number of AI self-driving cars is so tiny that no one would notice or care that they might not be able to do a drive-thru, but once AI self-driving cars start to become prevalent, I assure you the fast food companies would notice and create quite a stir.

Why would the fast food restaurants care? Imagine if you had a business that was going to essentially be blockaded and this blockading mechanism would not readily allow people to come to your business. You'd be pretty steamed about it. As I mentioned earlier, the drive-thru is an essential aspect of the fast food industry. If you inadvertently deprive the public at large of using a drive-thru, that's going to be a huge revenue blow to the fast food industry. You'd see those fast food places shrink and lots of employees laid-off.

Notice that I said that the AI self-driving cars might inadvertently be a form of blockade on this drive-thru matter. Unlike the earlier notion about purposely pre-programming AI self-driving cars to avoid a drive-thru, this is instead the circumstance that the AI self-driving car just doesn't know how to navigate a drive-thru. It's not yet been programmed to do so, because it's considered an edge or low priority problem, and thus the AI is unable to perform that particular driving task. Those that are again the ones that want to prevent AI self-driving cars from using a drive-thru would be thrilled to know that there's a chance that the AI self-driving cars might not be able to use a drive-thru simply because they aren't capable to do so.

I'm sure there are some AI developers reading this discussion right now that are besides themselves saying that they cannot imagine why an AI self-driving car cannot navigate a drive-thru. This seems on the surface like a very simple driving task. Heck, novice teenage drivers are able to even navigate a drive-thru. This must be a no-brainer. Shouldn't any AI that can otherwise drive a car on our streets be able to also navigate a drive-thru?

Yes and no.

Let's consider the nature of the driving task as it relates to a drive-thru.

Keep in mind too that an AI self-driving car generally consists of these key driving components (per my framework):

- Sensor data collection and interpretation

- Sensor fusion

- Virtual world model updating

- AI action planning

- Car controls commands issuance

I'd also like to mention that there are varying levels of self-driving cars. The topmost level, considered a Level 5, consists of an AI self-driving car that requires no human driver. The AI is supposed to be able to drive in whatever manner a human can drive a car. There are usually no brake pedals, no gas pedals, and no steering wheel provided inside of an AI self-driving car, since it is expected that there is not a human driver involved. For the self-driving cars less than a Level 5, it is required that a human driver be present at all times and ready to undertake the driving task. In fact, it is expected that the human driver is co-sharing the driving task with the AI, which I've pointed out many times is ripe for quite adverse consequences.

For the purposes of this discussion about drive-thru operations, I'm going to only focus on the Level 5 self-driving cars.

This is sensible since a self-driving car that's less than a Level 5 has as a requirement that there be a human driver present and able to drive the car. In that case, if the AI self-driving car lacked an AI capability to navigate a drive-thru, the AI would presumably just hand the controls over to the human upon arriving at a drive-thru location, and indicate to the human to proceed as desired, namely the human would then drive the drive-thru. Once the human completed this part of the driving journey and popped out of the other end of the drive-thru, the AI could then presumably indicate it would takeover the driving once again, on a co-shared basis, and proceed to whatever is the next destination such as home or batting practice.

Thus, herein the attention is toward the nature of the drive-thru driving task and how the AI could undertake such a task.

For a true Level 5 self-driving car, the AI would need to be able to entirely navigate the drive-thru and not at any time need to revert back to a human driver (since there isn't a human driver in the Level 5 self-driving car; or, even if one happens to be in the self-driving car, there is no provision and no expectation of them needing to drive the self-driving car, at any time, and indeed for none of the time).

Upon arriving at a drive-thru location, which the AI of a self-driving car would be able to achieve by the usual capabilities of navigating to a particular address, the various steps include:

- Arrive at drive-thru location

- Find the drive-thru entrance

- Enter into the drive-thru entrance

- Navigate the drive-thru to a menu board (wait)

- Navigate the drive-thru to an ordering station (wait)

59

- Navigate the drive-thru to an order payment window (wait)

- Navigate the drive-thru to an order pick-up window (wait)

- Navigate to the exit of the drive-thru

- Proceed henceforth on rest of driving journey

Those aforementioned steps are the general aspects of dealing with a drive-thru. There are lots of exceptions and other aspects, but let's put those aside for the moment and concentrate on the overarching elements.

I'll briefly walk you through each of the steps, providing an indication of why each such step is somewhat beyond the normal driving tasks that an AI self-driving car is prepared to undertake.

Finding the entrance for a drive-thru can be tricky.

There are usually signs that indicate where the entrance is. The visual sensors of the AI self-driving car will likely be able to detect these signs. This sign detection can be somewhat hard since the signs are not standardized, akin to street signs like speed limits signs and such that are relatively standardized. Instead, these drive-thru signs can be whatever size, shape, colors, etc. that the drive-thru operator has chosen to use.

The AI needs to be able to detect those signs and interpret the signs as to where the AI self-driving car is to go. This involves updating the virtual world model and the AI updating its action plan, along with issuing car controls commands such as drive ahead ten feet and turn the wheel so that the car ends-up between those two curbs at the drive-thru entrance.

Often, there is a menu board that is sitting astride of the drive-thru path and it is intended to provide the human with an indication of what food products are available for purchase. I'm going to assume for the moment that the AI self-driving car in this scenario has a human inside it and will consider later on herein the case of no human within and other such variations.

You might find of interest that the menu board is actually quite important for a drive-thru.

I'm sure you likely go to fast food restaurants and often order the same food items each time. Therefore, you tend to ignore the menu board. You might even have a hard time remembering what the menu board even looks like at your favorite fast food drive-thru. As such, you might be surprised to know that the menu board is considered essential by the fast food operators.

Studies show that the menu board can be a tremendous upsell motivator. The human going through a drive-thru sees the items shown on the menu board, and even if that person already has a particular order in mind, they are often sparked in the moment to increase their order. If you've been in a car with children, I assure you that the children often look at the menu board and excitedly want to order everything shown on the board. Those menu boards are more than decorations, they are key as a revenue maker for the fast food entity.

Usually, after the menu board or sometimes right at location of the menu board, there is an ordering station. This might consist of a microphone and speaker, along with sometimes an electronic display that can be used to show the order to the human in the car. In some cases, you need to drive further forward to get to the order station, which could also be one of the windows of the drive-thru.

After placing the order, a human driver then proceeds to a payment window. At the payment window, the human provides some form of payment, usually credit card, debit card, or cash. This window might also serve as the order delivery window. In many cases, the payment window is separate from the order delivery window. In that case, after paying, the driver needs to proceed forward to the delivery window.

Once at the delivery window, the human in the car awaits the order. This might also entail some discussion with the agent at the order window. Included in this discussion could be requests for utensils and other such items. It could also involve the human opting to change their order or make other special requests.

Once the food has been handed over to the human that's inside the car, the car usually then proceeds forward. There is usually an exit from the drive-thru. After getting to the exit point, the driver usually needs to look and make sure that they can further proceed. The exit from the drive-thru might end-up into a parking lot or at times might arrive at a street or similar roadway. The driver needs to be mindful that they are now entering into overall traffic.

This point about entering into overall traffic is somewhat important. Usually, once the human driver has initially entered into the drive-thru at the entrance, they are essentially in a "protected" area within the confines of the drive-thru operation. In that sense, there tends to be less traffic-oriented issues that can arise, versus when being immersed into a normal traffic situation. It's a kind of a special quiet zone, of sorts. Once the car has reached the exit of the drive-thru, all of the usual kinds of traffic dangers and considerations come back into play, and all bets are off.

In quick recap, the self-driving car has to find the proper entrance, and then do a series of proceeding forwards, encompassing stop-and-waits along the way, and then at the end of the path be ready to continue into typical roadway conditions.

There's also the twist that the drive-thru might already have other cars in the midst of the same process. Of which, some of those cars might be human driven and some of those cars might be AI self-driving cars. It presumably does not matter whether the cars in the path are human driven versus AI self-driving car driven, in the sense that the focus of the AI self-driving car herein would need to ensure that it does not hit any of those other cars and nor if possible get hit by any of those other cars.

One aspects about these other cars involved in the drive-thru process is the short distances between each car. Most of today's AI self-driving cars are not keen on being bumper-to-bumper with other cars. Humans are used to being within inches of other cars, sometimes nearly actually at the bumper of other cars. For most AI self-driving cars, the AI system has been developed to allow for a greater preference of distance between the self-driving car and other cars, doing so as a safety measure and also to cope with the variability involved in the self-driving car sensors and distances detection.

Presumably, the AI self-driving car can do a follow-the-leader approach of driving the drive-thru, merely detecting the car ahead and opting to generally follow that car. The other car would presumably be doing the same series of stop-and-wait positionings, which could aid the AI in ascertaining where each of those spots are. This though cannot be done blindly, so to speak, by the AI self-driving car, because the car ahead could have had other reasons to come to other stops-and-waits and it does not necessarily mean those are the proper spots for stops-and-waits.

When I mentioned earlier that the drive-thru path is generally a protected path, it was a generalization that must be taken with a grain of salt. There's a drive-thru nearby where I live that has a bit of a sidewalk-like path that cuts through the drive-thru of the fast food restaurant. This fast food restaurant is also just a block or so anyway from a large high school. If you attempt to do the drive-thru just after the high school lets out, upon entering into the fast food drive-thru, you need to be watching out for a seemingly endless stream of high school students walking along that sidewalk, blocking your efforts to proceed forward in the drive-thru path.

Thus, the AI self-driving car needs to be alert to the potential of pedestrians while the self-driving car is navigating the drive-thru.

Of course, most drive-thru operations don't permit pedestrians to come up to the drive-thru windows, and so it is generally a rarity to have to deal with pedestrians while navigating a drive-thru in your car. It can happen, though, and the AI needs to be prepared to cope with the perhaps sudden and at times erratic behavior of pedestrians that could invade the drive-thru path.

There are some other interesting exceptions or special cases involved in a drive-thru. One time, I was at the tail end of the drive-thru, which was otherwise packed with a line of cars. As I came upon the drive-thru entrance and became the last car in sequence, for whatever reason, the car ahead of me suddenly put itself into reverse and started to back-up toward my car. I guess they didn't want to wait in the long time of cars, or maybe they decided it wasn't the kind of fast food they had a taste for at that time.

What would you do? You could of course refuse to also back-up. Tough luck for them that they decided to try and get out of the line. They could have just continued forward like the other cars, and declined to order anything, if they had decided they no longer wanted that particular fast food. I realize that if they opted to stay in line, they would need to wait their turn and that it would be frustrating for them, since they weren't actually presumably going to be ordering food. But, it would be a lot easier on everyone else if they had just proceeded forward in line, ordering or not, whichever they wished to do.

I looked behind my car and there weren't any other cars in line behind me. It was a bit dicey though that the entrance was preceded by a somewhat busy traffic area of a mall. I would be trying to back-up into a traffic lane. Other cars coming along would not be expecting a car to be backing out of the drive-thru area. There was a chance of my causing a collision or other calamity by trying to back my car out into the traffic lane. It seemed like a dangerous and somewhat unwarranted thing to do, and all the other car had to do was wait things out and proceed forward (I suppose you could say that maybe the other car had someone in it that had suffered a heart attack and they needed to urgently be rushed to the nearest hospital – well, I don't think that was the case and it appeared to be a bunch of teenage drivers that willy nilly had changed their minds).

I opted to back-up my car and let the other car out of the drive-thru path. Probably shouldn't have been so generous. Maybe they'll think they can do this same stunt as often as they like. For our herein purposes, the point is that there can be exceptions to the normal run-the-mill forward step-at-a-time progression of a drive-thru. Another special case are the drive-thru entrances that allow two cars to merge into one lane as they come into the drive-thru. That's another special handling circumstance. And so on.

You might be thinking that the driving of a drive-thru isn't that tough to figure out. Us humans do it all the time, and can come upon a drive-thru that we've never driven and be able to readily navigate it. This brings up the notion of Machine Learning (ML). It is conceivable that via the use of Machine Learning that you can have an AI self-driving car derive how to drive a drive-thru, after having undertaken the driving of some drive-thrus. In essence, the more drive-thrus you use, and if you are paying attention and learning from each instance, you can get better at navigating a drive-thru.

We are a big advocate of the use of ML for that purpose. It doesn't though negate the need to have the primitives already in-hand of how to navigate a drive-thru. In other words, you can't just unleash the AI self-driving car into the world and hope that it somehow figures out the drive-thru navigation. It is something that needs to be provided as a bootstrap. After which, the use of ML should be included to improve it's driving ability of the drive-thru operations over time.

I had mentioned earlier that a drive-thru might have other AI self-driving cars in line, in addition to human driven cars. Presumably, via the use of V2V (vehicle-to-vehicle communication), each of the AI self-driving cars can communicate electronically about being in the drive-thru line. For example, sometimes at certain times of the day, a drive-thru might close one of the windows and consolidate the ordering and payment and order delivery into the use of just one window. An AI self-driving car ahead of your AI self-driving car in the drive-thru line might be able to alert your AI self-driving car that there's just one window open.

So far, I've had an unspoken assumption in this discussion that the AI self-driving car contained human occupants, and that it would presumably be the human occupants involved in the ordering, payment, and food acceptance process. One aspect about true AI self-driving cars is that there is no requirement that a human occupant be inside of an AI self-driving car and that the AI self-driving car might be undertaking a journey without any human occupants involved per se.

You might be at home and decide that you are hungry for your favorite burger. Sure, you could hop into your AI self-driving car and tell it to go to the nearest fast food drive-thru. Or, instead, you might instruct your AI self-driving car to do so on your behalf. The driving aspects are the same regardless of whether you are in the self-driving car or not. The key change here would be that there's not a human in the self-driving car to indicate the order, provide payment, and nor receive the food.

With the emergence already of remote mobile ordering of fast food, the first two parts of the human-not-present are readily able to be handled. Assuming that the particular fast food restaurant you are interested in has already established mobile ordering, you can via your smartphone place your order, pay for it, and send your AI self-driving car along to do the pick-up for you. This could also entail that the AI self-driving car might not even go into the conventional drive-thru lane, since often times the fast food restaurants are arranging for a parking spot for mobile ordered food pick-up's.

In some manner, the AI self-driving car would need to be able to figure out where it needs to go once it arrives at the fast food restaurant, whether to navigate the drive-thru or go to an identified pick-up spot. This could be communicated by the fast food restaurant at the time that the order was placed, and the human using their smartphone might electronically convey as such to the AI self-driving car, or merely tell the AI self-driving car that it needs to go the parking space #82 when it arrives at the fast food joint.

Speaking of humans having to instruct an AI self-driving car, I am often asked why an AI self-driving car would need to be particularly pre-trained on navigating a drive-thru when it could presumably be coached by a human. In other words, suppose you are in an AI self-driving car and it has not ever navigated a Taco Bell drive-thru before. When it arrives at the Taco Bell, you could possibly tell the AI to go there to the marked entrance, move ahead and stop, move ahead some more, stop, wait, move ahead, etc. Thus, via human led instruction, you are guiding the AI self-driving car, and if the AI self-driving car is paying attention it would be using Machine Learning to be able to do the same drive-thru on its own on future occasions.

Yes, this notion of human led instruction is possible. It also tends to open a can of worms. Suppose a child is doing the instruction to the AI and therefore it is feasible that the instructions given are misleading or just outright wrong. Or, the manner of the natural language instructions are ambiguous and it is difficult for the AI to figure out what the human is actually instructing. Overall, it's a bit dicey to assume that human led instruction is going to be viable for an AI self-driving car. We'll need much heftier AI to be able to cope with human led instruction.

Another aspect of dealing with drive-thru operations will be the desire of the drive-thru owners to ensure that AI self-driving cars can readily and safely navigate the drive-thru. Obviously, the owners have a big motivation to make sure that AI driven cars can come to the drive-thru. As pointed out earlier, drive-thru is a significant chunk of the revenue of a fast food restaurant.

It is possible that drive-thru operations will willingly adjust their drive-thru operations to accommodate AI self-driving cars, especially if the AI of the AI self-driving cars is crude at dealing with a drive-thru or unable to do so on its own. Via adding various electronic communications devices, somewhat akin to the Internet of Things (IoT), the drive-thru could be transmitting instructions to an AI self-driving car regarding navigating the drive-thru.

Once the AI self-driving car arrives near the entrance of the drive-thru, the fast food restaurant might beam messages as to where the entrance is. The fast food drive-thru could then beam to the AI self-driving car that the car should proceed forward and stop, then proceed forward again, and so on. In this manner, it is almost like an airplane being at an airport. There is a kind of traffic controller that is providing instructions to the AI self-driving cars. This could be done nearly entirely by computer to computer aspects and no human intervention necessarily needed.

The need for a drive-thru to adjust and add the various IoT communicating instructions is an added cost to the drive-thru operation. As such, if you multiply that cost by the thousands upon thousands of drive-thrus in the United States, it could be quite a financial burden for the drive-thru owners. I'm sure the drive-thru owners would prefer to avoid that cost if possible. It would be considered better if the AI itself was strong enough that no such adjustments were needed. This same AI strength could come to play in many other circumstances too, beyond just navigating a drive-thru.

With the advent of AI self-driving cars there is also going to be increased availability of ridesharing. I'd be willing to bet that this will also mean that people will use a ridesharing service to sometimes bring them food from a fast food place (you are at home and request an AI self-driving car of a ridesharing service to pick-up some burgers for you). I'd also anticipate that with the advent of blockchain, it will be likely that the entire transaction occurs electronically in the cloud, and that your preferred order from fast food places would be stored in the blockchain too (in addition to paying for the food and for the rideshare ride).

In terms of the AI system being able to navigate a fast food drive-thru, there's a nearer term aid that the fast food places could also try. Rather than putting up various IoT devices at the fast food place to electronically communicate to the AI self-driving car, another approach would be to provide a set of instructions for an AI self-driving car. Those instructions could be shared with the AI self-driving car as a kind of overall guide about navigating the drive-thru. Those instructions aren't as capable as the real-time interactivity of IoT, but at least would provide some semblance of aid to the AI for navigating the drive-thru.

We're working on a protocol and templates for such purposes.

This would make it easy for any fast food chain to readily populate the template with the specifics for each of their fast food locations. These could then be fed into the AI self-driving cars. Indeed, it could be included in the cloud based system supporting the particular brand of AI self-driving cars, and via their OTA (Over The Air) updating process, they could download and make use of the instructions.

Will AI self-driving cars spell the death knell for drive-thru operations? Some believe that via the advent of AI self-driving cars that there won't even be any need for a drive-thru anymore, since instead the AI self-driving car would merely park and pick-up orders. Though this is a possibility, I'd bet that humans will still be interested in doing a drive-thru and not necessarily ordering their food in a remote fashion. We might eventually get there, but not in the nearer term.

There are some that hope that AI self-driving cars might put fast food restaurants out of business since it is believed that fast food is bad for us. I'd tend to believe that AI self-driving cars might actually aid fast food restaurants and make it even easier to get fast food. Indeed, there will likely be added pressure on conventional sit-down restaurants as it becomes easier for the public to opt toward fast food due to AI self-driving cars, and not want to contend with the logistics involved in sit-down eateries.

AI self-driving cars and drive-thru operations, for some people it will be a match made in heaven. We just need to make sure that the AI is capable enough to cope with a drive-thru. That's an order -- and would you like some ketchup with that?

CHAPTER 4
OVERWORKING
ON
AI SELF-DRIVING CARS

CHAPTER 4

OVERWORKING ON
AI SELF-DRIVING CARS

You have your sleeping bag at the office for those overnight non-stop coding deadlines that require you to work on the AI system until you get the particular component working right. Turns out, you've been using the sleeping bag quite a bit lately. Furthermore, you often find yourself telling friends that you cannot spare time to go with them to an evening excursion at the local pubs, due to having to stay at work. The moment you get to work in the morning, you are bombarded with tons of very intense coding to be done, and of course eating lunch at your desk is the only means to try and keep your head above water (no time to go out and get food or heaven forbid sit at a restaurant and eat lunch there). It's a do-or-die culture at the workplace and you are immersed in it up to your teeth.

Welcome to the typical workplace conditions for AI developers doing AI self-driving car systems work.

Now, I'm not suggesting that there aren't lots of other computer system developers in lots of other lines of work that aren't doing the same. There are. In fact, if you were to go from building to building in a place like Silicon Valley, you are likely to find tons of developers all suffering the same fate. Non-stop work. Huge pressures. Deadlines, deadlines, deadlines. And generally, no hope that it will let up.

I think we're all amenable somewhat to the notion that from time-to-time there is a need for "maximum effort" toward doing development work. Those temporary urgencies do arise.

Putting one's personal life on-hold to handle something truly needed at work is part-and-parcel of being in our profession. In some sense, it can almost even be something that you can later on brag about, hey, I did an all-nighter and lived to tell the tale. Some might even claim that it can make the rest of the time seem sweeter, in the sense that if you pushed hard on something a couple of months or weeks ago, changing back to a more measured pace seems "leisurely" in comparison.

But, the question arises, does an excessive overworking workplace lend itself to properly developing AI self-driving cars?

Keep in mind that AI self-driving cars are life-or-death systems. If we were to compare the normal everyday kind of system to the AI system of a self-driving car, I think it would be fair to claim that the self-driving car system has a somewhat higher onus in terms of being built for high reliability and safety. Sure, that accounting system you are coding might also need reliability and safety, but if it gets the credits and debits mixed-up due to an error or bug, this seems not quite as catastrophic as an AI self-driving car that rams into a wall or a pedestrian due to an error or bug.

Some years ago, when I started-up a new company for AI oriented systems development, our first major client necessitated that we work night and day to develop the system they wanted. It was crucial that we delivered to this client, otherwise gossip would have spread in the grapevine that we weren't good enough to be considered for other major engagements. In this case, it was an AI system that pushed the limits of AI at the time. This made it doubly tough since we were trying to invent new Machine Learning (ML) techniques while also figuring out how to apply them to the particular need of the client.

As the founder and head of the company, I was knee deep in helping do the development (it wasn't until later on, once the company had grown that I was able to step back from the development efforts and take on the more all-encompassing role of leader and also rainmaker). The team that I had hired was surprised that I was sitting there cranking out code with them. They were more used to managers that would assign work to be done, rather than they themselves getting into the weeds. I was at that time willing to do anything and whatever it took to get our first big project delivered on-time and on-target to what was promised.

I felt bad about having my team have to work so hard and non-stop. Some of them had just started a family and were sacrificing time toward their significant other and their newborn kids. Some of them were eager to do the work and excited about being on the ground floor of something new. There was a wide range of reactions to the crazy blitz of work. I had pledged that it wouldn't last and that this was just being done to achieve a specific goal. Indeed, after we got the project completed successfully, I paid out a generous bonus to the team members and the next projects were less overwhelming in terms of work time.

Turns out that many companies today have taken the perspective that there is no end in sight for doing overwhelming work. It is the work. It is the standard practice at the company. I know many CEO's that brazenly tell everyone that they intentionally work their people the hardest of any other company in town. It's a source of pride to be able to say that you don't allow your team members to take vacation. These CEO's are proud to exclaim that they work their people to the bone.

Some even smirk that the appearance of providing perks at the office such as an in-house chef and ping pong tables is actually is a "trick" to keep their employees working at the office, done under the guise of claiming to show regard for their people. The minimal cost to provide food at the office is well-worth the added productivity of the developers. Keep those developers coding and doing so by throwing them a bone of one kind or another is easy enough to do.

Plus, the advent of smartphones and the Internet has made things even "better" for those companies desiring to wring every ounce out of their developers. An employee that leaves the office is still on-the-hook for answering questions and remaining engaged in work activities, via the use of their smartphone and their tablets. Texts galore, phone calls, the use of productivity tools such as Slack, and so on, all of which allow for true 24x7 work activity. In one sense, it doesn't matter if you are sitting at work or not per se (so-called "butts in seats"), since any moment that you are anywhere, the expectation can be that you'll respond and keep up with the ongoing work streams.

One company had encouraged their team members to "take a break" by heading to Yosemite (a wilderness area in Northern California, which is about a 3 ½ drive from Silicon Valley). Wow, unbelievable that the Attila the Hun leadership would actually encourage the developers to take some time off. Had the world come to an end?

Well, turns out that the company had arranged for the team members to stay in lodges at a camp area that was outfitted with Internet access. Yes, you guessed right if you deduced that the team members ended-up spending most of the time "in the wild" by sitting at the campground and working on their laptops. Furthermore, the leadership went too, ostensibly to also enjoy the outdoors, but more so to make sure that the team members were working and not taking time to go sightseeing. Now that's a quite a vacation!

So, is it sensible to go ahead and work your people non-stop or not?

Some would say that it has become the default practice. If your firm doesn't do this, other firms will, and those other firms will be able to get ahead of your firm. You can't "afford" to not have a non-stop work environment. Not only will your firm fall behind, there's the danger that your firm will become known for having slackers. Don't go to work at that place, it's the lazy developers that go there. Those wimps. They only produce a fraction of what other firms can get done in the same length of time.

There are many executives that believe utterly in the coding until-you-drop type of work environment. Furthermore, if you do drop, the viewpoint is that it shows your weakness. It shows that you aren't suitable for the big time. In a Darwinian way, these executives want just the survivors to be at their workplace. Survival of the fittest. And how to determine who is the fittest? Work, work, work. The ones left standing are the fittest. The ones that cannot stand it, they are out.

Drop them like a brick. It's as easy as that.

Sometimes these same executives will momentarily seemingly open their eyes to the situation and maybe, just maybe, concede that things are a bit over-the-top in terms of the workplace demands. Sadly, some of those will then do the Yosemite kind of trips under the false belief it will "refuel, recharge, and reconnect" their developers. They are either deluded into believing that a working "vacation" gets the trick done, or they know it won't but want to at least seem to be doing something about workplace complaints or qualms by those being overworked.

What does this have to do with AI self-driving cars?

At the Cybernetic AI Self-Driving Car Institute, we are developing AI systems for self-driving cars. As such, we keep tabs on what other like firms are doing, and we've had many of their AI developers that have eyed coming to us, based on the excessive overwork taking place at those other firms and the more measured tone that we take.

This brings up some important points about excessive overwork. Thought at first glance it might seem "wise" to overwork your AI developers, since it would appear to gain you some kind of efficiency and productivity gains, the surface level perspective can differ from the reality of what actually turns out.

Let's consider some of the downsides of the excessive overwork situation.

First, let's agree that people can get burned out at work. I've seen this happen many times at the numerous companies that I've worked at over the years. For AI developers, you can pretty quickly see them become less productive. They become more irritable and less collaborative. Since many computer people are already a bit cynical, you start to burn out one and I assure the cynicism goes through the roof. This can have a very negative result on their coding and development efforts, including the fostering of an "I could care less" attitude of whether some AI component works right or not.

This is a dangerous thing to ferment when you are developing AI software for self-driving cars.

I challenge you to demonstrate that a burnt-out AI developer is somehow highly efficient and productive, which is what the excessive overwork pundits might claim. Sure, you are getting those developers to work longer hours than someone in a less obsessed work-hours environment, but going toe-to-toe, does the additional hours really translate into being more efficient and productive. I'd say it does not.

See if you follow this kind of thinking. Suppose I have a worker that can produce 10 widgets per hour. Let's assume that after some number of hours Q, their productivity falls to 8 widgets per hour due to fatigue and other factors. Then, after some number of hours S, it falls to 4 widgets per hour. And so on. Also, after an accumulated number of hours T, the normal productivity of 10 widgets per hour falls to an ongoing lower level since the burn-out is having an sustaining and permanent productivity drain.

You can calculate out the aspect that over some length of time of being in an excessive overwork situation, the worker is eventually going to drop their productivity levels such that they become ultimately less productive than the not-so-overworked worker.

That's what some of these excessive overwork pundits fail to see. They think that the productivity remains high, regardless of whether you work one hour, 40 hours, 60 hours, or 80 hours. There's not much credence for such a belief. If you were working on an assembly line in a manufacturing plant, maybe this could be shown to somehow workout, but when you are doing sophisticated work like AI development, it's not the same as an assembly line (though at times it feels as merciless!).

So, the first principle here is that by working your AI developers toward excessive overwork you are burning them out, which will undermine productivity. Thus, you are falsely believing that by your people working more hours than other firms that you are somehow getting ahead of those other firms. It's a myth.

Second, the odds are pretty high that you'll have those AI developers seeking to leave your firm, doing so in hopes of finding a work environment of a more measured nature. This seems especially true for the millennial generation that is aiming to have a more balanced work/life portfolio. It's not that they aren't willing to work, it's that they are desirous of having work that can allow for life outside work too. One might claim that the prior generation(s) were taught to do whatever was needed for work, no questions asked, though this was also in a work climate of having companies that were more determined to provide career-long opportunities. This doesn't seem to be the case anymore. It's a mercenary work world nowadays, for both employers and employees.

I realize you might be thinking that having AI developers leave due to excessive overwork is just fine because they were the "weak" ones anyway. You might want to reconsider that belief. There's lots of really good AI talent that knows they can command what the market will bear. There is a low supply of such talent. There is very high demand for such talent. Indeed, they are likely the first to leave since they know they can get something better elsewhere. If anything, it could be that the ones that stay are the "weaker" ones – though, I shun this whole idea of the weak versus the strong and don't want to get mired in that debate herein.

Third, if you have a high churn rate on your AI team, it will definitely adversely impact the systems being developed for an AI self-driving car.

Each time you have one of your AI developers leave, the odds are that whatever portion they were working on will now suffer falling behind or have other maladies. Plus, whomever you hire has to initially go up a learning curve of whatever is being worked on. Therefore, you are going to take a big productivity hit during the time that the AI developer was gone after leaving the firm, and until the new hire gets fully up-to-speed.

These could be significant chunks of time. From the moment that an AI developer leaves your team, until the time that you've found a suitable replacement, and brought that replacement on-board, and given them a reasonable amount of time to figure out what the predecessor was working on, I'd dare say it could be many weeks and in some cases months to do so.

You also need to consider the impact to the AI development team. The odds are that you'll use some of them to aid in the interviewing process. Count that as lost productivity towards their AI development tasks. Once you hire the replacement, the odds are that other members of the team will need to aid bringing that person up-to-speed. More lost productivity for them. Imagine too if the replacement turns out to not be conducive to the rest of the team, and so it could be that you might have harmed the overall productivity of the entire team for a long time.

Another factor of excessive overwork involves error rates and can severely undermine the safety and reliability of the AI self-driving car systems.

Suppose I can produce 100 lines of code per hour. A colleague, Joe, let's say he also produces 100 lines of code per hour. We seem to have the same productivity rate. Imagine that my code is completely error free (yay!). Imagine that Joe has 1 error per every 20 lines of code. To deal with the errors, there will be time needed to find them and correct them. And, that presumes you can even find the errors.

This is illustrating that you need to consider the error rates and other such factors and not fall into the trap of relying upon some other simplistic measure of however you count productivity. AI self-driving cars need to have highly reliable systems. There needs to be overt and ongoing and insistent efforts toward making the AI system be as reliable and safe as feasible. Not doing so will likely produce AI systems that are more so error prone, leading to a possibly disastrous result for all.

I'd like to also toss into the excessive overwork scenario that it can lead to bad decisions about crucial design elements of an AI system. It can cause the members of the team to become so stressed that they make takeout their frustrations by purposely undermining the AI system, maybe even seeding something dastardly into it. Some at times have turned to drugs to try and maintain the non-stop work efforts, which then can lead to an undermining of their lives both inside and outside of work. Etc.

Here's another sometimes shocking surprise to those leaders that think they are doing the right thing by promoting a company culture of excessive overwork, namely the fake work approach. An AI developer can be clever enough to appear to be making progress when they are really just doing fake work. If you come to me and ask me for an estimate of how long it will take to setup that ML portion for a particular component, I might sandbag you by giving you a super high estimate. I do so to protect myself secretly from the overwork. This seems sensible to the worker because they feel that if the firm is being unfair to them, why not be unfair in return.

I am guessing that some of you might be thinking that this discussion about excessive overwork is a plea to go toward being underworked. Lance, are you saying that my people should lounge near the pool during the workday, drinking margaritas, and having a good old time, and punch the clock once and a while. No, I'm not saying that. If that's what you think I'm saying, please take off those rose-colored glasses about the fantastic advantages of excessive overwork that you seemed to believe in. Time to smell the coffee and wake-up to what's really happening by your approach.

Notice that I've tried to carefully phrase the nature of the overwork as "excessive" in the sense that I am saying taking overwork to an extreme is the problem.

As I earlier mentioned, doing overwork is often a needed element when facing particular deadlines. This though is typically temporary in nature and the AI developers can stretch to cope with it, knowing that they will not be mired in it permanently.

For some high-tech leaders that romanticize excessive overwork, I think if they really looked closely at the impact it is having on their teams, they might reconsider whether their high-level perspective matches with reality.

Others in the firm will often act as "yes men" to go along with the excessive overwork philosophy, since the top leader won't consider anything else but it. For those firms headed by the "excessive overwork" demanding take-no-prisoners leader, it's hard to get those kinds of personalities to see anything other than the advantages of insisting on excessive overwork.

Let's just hope that the AI self-driving cars under their tutelage don't come back to harm us all if those AI systems are "wimpy" in comparison to the stronger and safer such systems developed in a more measured work environment.

CHAPTER 5

SLEEPING BARBER PROBLEM
AND
AI SELF-DRIVING CARS

CHAPTER 5

SLEEPING BARBER PROBLEM AND AI SELF-DRIVING CARS

The sleeping barber problem. It's a classic. If you are unfamiliar with it, you might be thinking that I've somehow got a barber that falls asleep when I come in to get my haircut. That would indeed be a problem. Just imagine the kind of haircut I might get if the barber kept falling asleep during the haircut. It would take a long time to get my haircut done, and it might look like it was done in a series of staggered steps. Fortunately, that's not the sleeping barber problem that I'm referring to.

Well known among computer scientists and especially those that study real-time systems, the sleeping barber problem dates back to the mid-1960s when famous computing enthusiast Edsger W. Dijkstra (known generally be his initials of EWD), depicted the problem for purposes of exploring how to handle various concurrent programming related issues. If you aren't aware of EWD's body of work, his efforts were of a pioneering nature and we all today utilize daily in our computer efforts the insights that he gleaned.

I met EWD a few times at industry events, and true to his reputation he was a bit gruff and had little patience for those that weren't up-to-par. He had made a choice via advice from a mentor to earlier in his career switch from his focus on physics to instead focus on providing rigor to what at the time was a Wild West of computer programming. Thankfully he made the switch. He was also well known for a disdain for the phrase "computer science" and instead insisted that if this emerging field of study was going to be named that at least it be called "computing science" (you might have heard his famous line, namely that computer science is no more about computers than is astronomy about telescopes).

Let's take a look at the sleeping barber problem.

Imagine that there's a barber willing to cut people's hair. The barber cuts only one person's hair at a time. There is one barber's chair. Once the barber starts to cut someone's hair, the barber sees it to the end of the haircutting for that person. The barber never directly turns away someone that wants a haircut if the barber is available to cut someone's hair.

If the barber believes that there is no one desiring a haircut, the barber will go to sleep, doing so in the barber's chair. If someone arrives at the barber's door and wants a haircut and the barber is asleep, the barber has a sixth sense and will awaken in order to cut that person's hair. When the barber first arrives to open the barbershop, the barber opens up the shop and sits in the barber chair and falls asleep, ostensibly to await for a customer that wants a haircut.

As an aside, yes, I realize that this barber might end-up getting a lot of sleep during a workday, but hey, that's fine and don't we all need naps during our workdays?

From time-to-time, people will arrive in an effort to get their haircut undertaken. There's just the one barber (we can complicate things with more than one barber, but the foundational problem is sufficient to concentrate on just having one barber). There is a waiting room into which the people desiring a haircut will ultimately wait, if a wait is needed and possible. In the waiting room, there is some limited number of seats, which I'll go ahead and call N.

The barber's chair and where the haircutting is taking place is apart from the area where the waiting room is. I mention this because it's a significant element to the nature of the problem. Many might assume that the waiting area and the haircutting area are all in the same physical space, such that those sitting waiting can watch the haircutting, and the barber can watch those that are waiting for a haircut. We're not going to have this kind of a setup in the case of the sleeping barber problem. Instead, consider that the haircutting room is disjointed from the waiting room and that you can't see either one from the other one. I know this seems odd in comparison to most actual barbershops, but hey, go with me on this assumption, thanks.

By the way, there are lots of online videos that try to explain the sleeping barber problem. Please be aware that many of them, even the most popular ones, either do a lousy job of explaining the problem, or fail to explain the solution, or explain the solution in a lopsided manner. I am hoping that my explanation herein will be better than those attempts by others. When I used to describe the problem and solution as a professor, I did my best to make clear cut to the students what the problem is and what the solutions consist of.

I'll say one other thing. For computer practitioners, they often glaze over in the eyes when I start to describe the sleeping barber problem. I don't blame them. There are various at times obscure "problems" in the computer science field and would rarely apply to the everyday efforts of a typical computer programmer or software engineer. In this case, though, I assure you that the sleeping barber problem has real-world practical implications and it's worthwhile to know about it. Really, I swear to you that's the case.

Okay, back to the problem description. One barber. Willing to cut hair. People come to get their haircut. These prospective customers will first go to the haircutting room to see if the barber is available. They'll know the barber is available because the barber will be sleeping when otherwise not cutting hair. If the barber is cutting hair when the prospective customer comes to look and see if the barber is available, the customer will then mosey on over to the waiting room, which takes a bit of time to wander over to (recall that the haircutting room and the waiting room are apart from each other).

A prospective customer that has seen that the barber is cutting hair and therefore busy, once that prospective customer gets to the waiting room they will try to sit down in an available seat. If all of the seats are taken, the prospective customer leaves. They might or might not return at some later point in time, which for purposes of the problem we don't care per se whether a "spurned" prospective customer opts to return later or not.

I suppose you could say that the barber ought to incentivize someone to come back to get a haircut if the person was unable to wait in the waiting room. Sure, that would be handy if this were more of a business-oriented problem rather than a computer science problem. We'll stay with the computer science focus for the moment.

You might be wondering how the people in the waiting room are going to become aware when the barber is available to cut their hair. The barber upon finishing cutting of someone's hair will proceed over to the waiting room to see if someone is waiting. If there is someone waiting, the barber then brings them over into the haircutting room and proceeds to cut their hair. If there is no on sitting in the waiting room, the barber will simply return to the haircutting room and fall asleep in the barber's chair.

The barber cuts hair in some amount of time T, which can vary depending upon the nature of the haircut. A haircut cannot somehow be done instantaneously, such that there is no such thing as T=0. We don't know how much time T it takes for any given haircut and will just assume that it is some quantifiable amount of time, and for which too it is a bounded amount of time. In essence, T cannot be equal to infinite (i.e., haircuts are guaranteed to eventually be completed).

For those prospective customers that end-up in the waiting room, they are willing to wait as long as it takes to get a haircut. We could complicate matters by saying that they only will wait some limited amount of time, but for the foundational aspects we'll leave it that they'll just wait. Heck, maybe the barber has really good WiFi and so the waiting customers can use their smartphones and do streaming of their favorite shows.

I've provided so far the essence of the setup. I added a few elaborations and maybe a little humor to the description but figured it might make it less painful for your purposes of getting to know the key setup aspects.

Let's walk through some examples.

The barber shows-up at 7 a.m. and dutifully opens the barbershop, which includes opening the waiting room and opening the haircutting room. There are no prospective customers as yet. The barber goes into the haircutting room, sits in the barber's chair, and promptly goes to sleep. It could be that the barber already had a solid night's sleep and so really doesn't need more sleep, or it could be that the barber partied last night and hasn't gotten any sleep at all, having arrived at 7 a.m. from the bars and nightclubs, in any case, there's no customers and so the barber sleeps.

Let's next pretend that a prospective customer shows up. The prospective customer goes directly to the haircutting room, not yet having seen or been to the waiting room and looks in the haircutting room to see if the barber is available.

Since in this instance the barber is sleeping, it implies the barber is available. The barber via a sixth sense wakes-up and happily cuts the hair of this first customer. When the haircut is completed, the customer leaves and the barber goes back to sleep. The barber cut the hair of one person. There were no other people that arrived. There was no one in the waiting room.

Ka-ching, the barber just made some money (well, I admit that I never said whether the barber gets paid to do haircuts, and so maybe the barber does this for free; just wanted to see if you were paying attention as to what I might have left out, but we don't care herein whether the barber is getting paid or not).

Straightforward first example, I believe.

Another prospective customer arrives, goes to see if the barber is available, sees the barber sleeping, the barber awakens, and starts to cut the hair of this customer. During the haircut, another prospective customer arrives, and goes to the door of the haircutting room. Upon seeing the barber busily cutting hair, the customer then makes their way over to the waiting room. In this case, let's say there are 2 seats in the waiting room (thus, N=2). The prospective customer notices that both seats are empty and so opts to sit down in one of the seats. They now preoccupy themselves in whatever manner so desired and are waiting to get their haircut.

Upon completing the haircut that was underway, the barber says goodbye to the customer that quite enjoyed getting the haircut, and the barber then meanders over to the waiting room. Maybe the barber secretly hopes there's no one there, such that sleep would be possible. Or, maybe the barber is eager to work and is hoping that there's someone in the waiting room.

In this case, there is someone waiting in the waiting room. The barber brings along the waiting customer and takes the customer over into the haircutting room. The barber proceeds to cut their hair. While doing so, another prospective customer shows up, looks and sees that the barber is busy, goes over to the waiting room, sees the two available seats, and takes a seat. Furthermore, another prospective customer comes along, sees that the barber is busy, so goes to the waiting room and grabs the second seat. All seats in the waiting room are now full, for the moment.

This haircut is taking a while to do. Turns out another prospective customer comes along, sees that the barber is cutting hair, so goes over to the waiting room. Darn, all of the seats are taken by other waiting customers. Guess today was the wrong day to want a haircut. This now despondent prospective customer walks away, unhappy and wishing they had come sooner to get their haircut.

I think that's enough of an example to now reveal the problem at-hand.

The setup seems just fine. Putting aside the tidbits about possibly losing customers because of the limited wait room, let's focus on something else instead.

Sometimes when the problem itself is revealed, it seems almost like a cheat in that if the problem had been described in a different way that you might have already detected the potential problem. In this case, I gave some clues but not much. Sorry.

The problem has to do with time.

We have the time it takes to do a haircut. There's also an unstated amount of time for the barber to walk over to the waiting room to see if there's anyone in there. There's more unstated time, such as the time it takes for a prospective customer to walk over to the waiting room once they have seen that the barber is busy.

Remember that it was mentioned that the haircutting room and the waiting room are apart from each other, and that you cannot see the room from the other room. Let's also go with the idea that the path from the haircutting room to the waiting room can be convoluted and such that someone on that path does not see anyone else on that path, even if there is someone else on the path.

This then is the problem.

A prospective customer arrives and let's say sees that the barber is busy, and so wanders over to the waiting room, which will take some amount of time, Z. Suppose the barber finishes the haircut just moments after that prospective customer has proceeded toward the waiting room, and meanwhile the barber has a faster way to get to the waiting room and so zooms over to see if there is anyone waiting. At that moment in time, there isn't anyone in the waiting room, even though we know that there's someone on their way to it. The barber though sees that the waiting room is empty, and so goes back to the haircutting room and will promptly go to sleep because there aren't any customers (as far as the barber knows).

The prospective customer finally arrives at the waiting room. They sit down. They are unaware that the barber came over to check and see whether anyone was there. This prospective customer assumes that the barber is still cutting the hair of the person that they saw when having come to the haircutting room door. We've said that the prospective customer is willing to wait until the barber becomes free, which will only be known when the barber comes to the waiting room.

But, we now have a conundrum.

The barber is sleeping and doesn't believe that there is anyone in the waiting room. The prospective customer that is patiently sitting in the waiting room is willing to just sit there, happily awaiting the presumed arrival at some point in time of the barber to then proceed with getting a haircut. Neither one realizes that they are both now waiting. You might say this is like waiting for Godot (a literary joke, if I might!). They will both presumably wait until forever, or maybe once the cows come home.

There are other variants on the problem, all of which involve time.

In the computing field, there are circumstances wherein you might have one process, in this sleeping barber case embodied in the notion of the barber, and you might have another process, in this case embodied in the customer that's waiting for the barber, whereby the two processes get themselves into a similar mess. Each might be waiting on the other, not realizing that they are indeed waiting on each other.

Suppose my PC tries to connect with my printer. The printer is momentarily busy because it is in the midst of printing a document. The PC upon inquiring of the printer is told by the printer that it is busy and so if the PC wants to send another document to the printer, the PC will need to wait until the printer is finished printing the being printed document. The PC is a bit slow and while it is digesting the aspect that the printer is busy, the printer actually finishes printing and tries to let the PC know. The PC though has finally gotten squared away that the printer is busy and so subsequently is going to wait until the printer says it is not busy.

You could end-up in a situation wherein the PC believes it is waiting for the printer, and the printer believes it is waiting for the PC. The document that you wanted to get printed is now in limbo, due to the aspect that these two processes got themselves out-of-synch and are doing a lousy job of inter-process communication.

At the heart of any solid operating system is the ability to cope with synchronization among multiple processes and trying to ensure that there is proper inter-process communications taking place. If an OS doesn't' have its act together on dealing with this, you are going to have all sorts of problems ensue related to the running of processes.

What does this have to do with AI self-driving cars?

At the Cybernetic AI Self-Driving Car Institute, we are developing AI software for self-driving cars. As such, one of the crucial elements for any self-driving car involves the proper design and development of the AI so that the multitude of processes and the appropriate synchronization and inter-process communication occurs, all of which has to happen in real-time and in the right manner.

In that sense, there's a chance that a poorly designed or insufficiently developed AI self-driving car could find itself mired in the sleeping barber problem. Shouldn't happen. Better not happen. Lives could depend upon it not happening.

There are some key overall tasks that occur by the AI to undertake the driving task, which includes:

- Sensor data collection and interpretation
- Sensor fusion
- Virtual world model updating
- AI action planning
- Car controls command issuance

Suppose that we have an AI self-driving car that's considered to be at Level 5. A Level 5 self-driving car is one that is driven entirely by the AI and there is no need and no provision for a human driver. In fact, a Level 5 self-driving car will usually lack a brake pedal, nor have a gas pedal, nor a steering wheel, since those are contraptions only needed for a human driver. AI self-driving cars that are less than a Level 5 are considered being co-driven by a human driver and the AI, and therefore will have the usual mechanisms needed for a human driver to participate in the driving task. This co-sharing of the driving task raises some serious and disconcerting potential problems.

Imagine a Level 5 self-driving car that is driving along on a highway. It's nighttime. The AI is using its sensors to try and detect the surroundings of the self-driving car. Using the cameras, the radar, the LIDAR, the sonic sensors, the AI is receiving data about what the sensors are detecting. Because it is nighttime, the road ahead is somewhat obscured by darkness, thus the cameras aren't as readily able to visually detect the scene ahead as if it were daylight. The radar becomes perhaps especially important in this setting.

At a speed of say 50 miles per hour, the self-driving car is moving along at a clip of about 75 feet per second. If the AI determines that there is a pedestrian up ahead and in the path of the self-driving car, it will need time to issue commands to the car controls, such as braking the car, and then it will take time for the car to actually come to a stop once the braking operation is enacted.

Let's assume that the AI checks with the sensor detection process and requests whether there is a pedestrian up ahead (at least as can be detected within the distance limitations of the sensors and the circumstances of the in-motion car). It could be that the sensor detection process indicates there isn't a pedestrian up ahead.

The AI opts to proceed with other driving tasks and for the moment believes that there is not a pedestrian up ahead.

Meanwhile, the sensor detection process receives a new set of data coming from the sensors, and upon analysis determines there now might be a pedestrian up ahead. It could be that a moment ago, the sensor data had been too sketchy and there was noise in it, so determining that a pedestrian was present was not readily feasible, a moment ago. Or, it could be that the self-driving car has moved forward at the 75 feet per second and it now has gotten closer to a pedestrian that was there in the street before but was outside the range of the sensors, a moment ago. Or, it could be that the pedestrian was not in the street before, but in the moment since the last sensor data collection, the pedestrian has rushed into the street and now is in front of the approaching AI self-driving car.

Here's your worst fears. The AI overarching process is still operating under the indication there isn't a pedestrian up ahead. The sensor detection process now believes that a pedestrian is up ahead. Suppose that the AI overarching process was designed so that it will assume there isn't a pedestrian until the sensor detection process alerts the AI overarching routine that there is one there. Suppose the sensor detection process was designed so that it waits until the AI overarching process asks about pedestrian detections.

You could now have one process that's waiting on the other, but the other one doesn't realize it is being waited upon.

By the time that the AI overarching process checks in with the sensor detection process, it might now be too late. Even if the AI overarching process now realizes that it is crucial to brake the self-driving car, the amount of time needed to issue the car controls commands and have the car respond, well, it could be that the pedestrian is going to get hit.

In case you think that something like this would certainly never happen, you might want to take a look at the Uber AI self-driving car incident that occurred in Arizona and involved the self-driving car hitting and killing a pedestrian. We don't yet know the inner workings of what actually happened, since it hasn't been made public, but something like this timing matter might have been involved. It could be a variant of the sleeping barber problem.

Let's now return to the sleeping barber problem.

You might be wondering what kind of solutions there are for the sleeping barber problem.

The solution that is one of the most commonly used approaches involves making use of two techniques in combination with each other.

One technique involves the use semaphores, which are essentially flags to indicate some kind of status, and the other technique used in combination with semaphores is usually mutual exclusion (often abbreviated as "mutex").

Mutual exclusion consists of a process that can claim exclusive control over something and any other process is prevented from trying to control that something (during that time period of exclusivity). We might therefore setup a semaphore that indicates the status of the waiting room, and have the barber momentarily acquire control over that status when it wants to check and see if there are any customers in the waiting room. This same semaphore could be used by a prospective customer that is able to gain control over it, momentarily, and check the status.

Without getting too deep into the details, this approach typically requires three semaphores, including one that is a count of the number of customers in the waiting room, another is whether the barber is cutting hair or not, and the third is used for the mutex status. If you are interested in the various solutions and sample source code, you can readily find online the code in numerous programming languages, including Python, Java, C++, and so on.

The addition of mutual exclusion requires that the processes each have a specific portion that deals with the mutual exclusion activity. This code segment is often referred to as a critical section. The critical section is usually supposed to be very short and quick to operate. When the overall process is doing its thing, considered its overall non-critical section, and wants to involve the mutex, it needs to make a request to do so, and goes into a waiting mode until granted the mutex control, and once it has completed the mutex activity it is expected to then release the control.

There are various potential problems associated with the mutual exclusion solution. One is that the waiting time for the mutex control might be inordinately long, while another concern is that whomever gets the mutex control might fail to release it. Each of these can create various forms of deadlock. There are other solutions associated with dealing with the deadlocks.

For AI developers that have developed real-time systems for say robots, they likely have had to deal with these kinds of sleeping barber problems, and therefore are familiar with how to develop their systems accordingly. On the other hand, for AI developers that have not done much work on real-time systems, they are often unfamiliar with these kinds of issues.

I mention this because the auto makers and tech firms are using a variety of AI developers, some that are familiar with these kinds of real-time issues and others that are no quite so familiar with it. Indeed, there are some AI developers that just assume that the underlying operating system will take care of any of these kinds of process synchronization and inter-process communications aspects. That can be a faulty assumption.

An AI self-driving car is a real-time system that needs to operate with often dozens of core processes occurring concurrently, possibly even hundreds of processes and thousands of mini-processes overall occurring simultaneously, and there needs to be an appropriate design and coding for their synchronization and inter-process communication.

The complexity of the AI for a self-driving car can become so thorny that it's difficult to know for sure that there aren't potential sleeping barbers hidden within the system. If a crucial "barber" gets confused or is not timely updated, the action of the self-driving car can become quite untoward. Life or death of humans can depend on how well the barber sleeping problem has been solved for an AI self-driving car.

CHAPTER 6

SYSTEM LOAD BALANCING
AND
AI SELF-DRIVING CARS

CHAPTER 6

SYSTEM LOAD BALANCING
AND
AI SELF-DRIVING CARS

The other day, my children decided to cook a meal in our kitchen and went whole hog into the matter (so to speak). I'm not much of a cook and tend to enjoy eating a meal more so than the labor involved in preparing a meal. In this case, it was exciting to see the joy of the kids as they went about putting together a rather amazing dinner. Perhaps partially due to watching the various chef competitions on TV and cable, and due to their own solo cooking efforts, when they joined together it was a miraculous sight to see them bustling about in the kitchen in a relatively professional manner.

I mainly aided by asking questions and serving as a taste tester. From their perspective, I was more of an interloper than someone actually helping to progress the meal making process. One aspect that caught my attention was the use of our stove top. The stove top has four burner positions. On an everyday cooking process, I believe that four heating positions is sufficient. I could see that with the extravagant dinner that was being put together, the fact that there were only four available was a constraint. Indeed, seemingly a quite difficult constraint.

During the cooking process, there were quite a number of pots and pans containing food that needed to be heated-up. I'd wager that at one point there were at least a dozen of such pots and pans in the midst of containing food and requiring some amount of heating. Towards the start of the cooking, it was somewhat manageable because they only were using three of the available heating spots. By using just three, it allowed them to then allocate one spot, the fourth one, as an "extra" for round robin needs. For this fourth spot, they were using it to do quick warm-ups and meanwhile the other three spots were for truly doing a thorough cooking job that required a substantive amount of dedicated cooking time.

Pots and pans were sliding on and off that fourth spot like a hockey puck on ice. The other three spots had large pots that were gradually each coming to a bubbling and high-heat condition. When one of the three pots had cooked well enough, the enterprising cooks took it off the burner almost immediately and placed it onto a countertop waiting area they had established for super-heated pots and pans that could simmer for a bit.

The moment that one pot came off of any of the three spots, another one was instantly put into its place. Around and around this went, in a dizzying manner as they contended with only having four available heating spots. They kept one spot in reserve and used it for more of a quick paced warm-up and had opted to use the other three for deep heated cooking. As they neared the end of the cooking process for this meal, they began to use nearly all of the spots for the quick paced warm-up needs, apparently because they had by then done the needed cooking already and no longer needed to devote any of the pots to a prolonged period on a heating spot.

As a computer scientist at heart, I was delighted to see them performing a delicate dance of load balancing. You've probably had situations involving multiple processors or maybe multiple web sites wherein you had to do a load balance across them. In the case of web sites, it's not uncommon for some popular web sites to be replicated at multiple geographic sites around the world, allowing for more ready speed responses to those from that part of the world. It also can help when one part of the world starts to bombard one of your sites and you need to flatten out the load else that particular web site might choke due to the volume.

In the cooking situation, the kids realized that having just four burner stove top positions was insufficient for the true amount of cooking that needed to take place for the dinner. If they had opted to sequentially and serially have placed pots of food onto the burners in a one-at-a-time manner, they would have had some parts of the meal cooked much earlier than other parts of the meal. In the end, when trying to serve the meal, it would have been a nightmarish result of some food that had been cooked earlier and was now cold, and perhaps other parts of the meal that were superhot and would need to wait to be eaten.

If the meal had been one involving much less preparation, such as if they had only three items to be cooked, they would have readily been able to use the stove top without any of the shenanigans of having to float around the pots and pans. They could have just put on the three pots and then waited until the food was cooked. But, since they had more needs for cooking then just the available heating spots, they needed to devise a means to make use of the constrained resources in a manner that would still allow for the cooking process to proceed properly.

This is what load balancing is all about. There are situations wherein there are a limited available supply of resources, and the number of requests to utilize those resources might exceed the supply. The load balancer is a means or technique or algorithm or automation that can try to balance out the load.

Another valuable aspect of a load balancer is that it can try to even out the workload, which might help in various other ways. Suppose that one of the stove tops was known to sometimes get a bit cantankerous when it is on high-heat for a long time. One approach of a load balance might be to try and keep that resource from peaking and so purposely adjust to use some other resource for a while.

We can also consider the aspect of resiliency. You might have a situation wherein one of the resources might unexpectedly go bad or otherwise not be usable. Suppose that one of the burners broke down during the cooking process. A load balance would try to ascertain that a resource is no longer functioning, and then see if it might possible to shift the request or consumption over to another resource instead.

Being a load balancer can be a tricky task.

Suppose the kids had decided that they would keep one of stove top burners in reserve and not use it unless it was absolutely necessary. In that case, they might have opted to use the three other burners in a manner of allocating two for the deep heating and one for the warming up. All during this time, the other fourth burner would remain unused, being held in reserve. Is that a good idea?

It depends. I'd bet that the cooking with just the three burners would have stretched out the time required to cook the dinner. I can imagine that someone waiting to eat the dinner might become disturbed if they saw that there was a fourth burner that could be used for cooking, and yet it was not, and the implication being that the hungry person had to wait longer to eat the dinner. This person might go ballistic that a resource sat unused for that entire time. What a waste of a resource, it would seem to that person.

Imagine further if at the start of the cooking process we were to agree that there should be an idle back-up for each of the stove burners being used. In other words, since we only have four, we might say that two of the burners will be active and the other two are the respective back-up for each of them. Let's number the burners as 1, 2, 3, and 4. We might decide that burner 1 will be active and it's back-up is burner 2, and burner 3 will be active and its back-up is burner 4.

While the cooking is taking place, we won't place anything onto the burners 2 and 4, until or if a primary of the burners 1 or burner 3 goes out. We might decide to keep the back-up burners entirely turned-off, in which case as a back-up they would be starting at a cold condition if we needed to suddenly switch over to one of them. We might instead agree that we'll go ahead and put the two back-ups onto a low-heat position, without actually heating anything per se, and generally be ready then to rapidly go to high-heat if they are needed in their back-up failover mode.

I had just now said that burner 2 would be the back-up for primary burner 1. Suppose I adhered to that aspect and would not budge. If burner 3 went suddenly out and I reverted to using burner 4 as the back-up, but then somehow burner 4 went out, should I go ahead and use burner 2 at that juncture? If I was insistent that burner 2 would only and always be a back-up exclusively for burner 1, presumably I would want the load balancer to refuse to now use burner 2, even though burners 3 and 4 are kaput. Maybe that's a good idea, maybe not.

These are the kinds of considerations that go into establishing an appropriate load balancer. You need to try and decide what the rules are for the load balancer. Different circumstances will dictate different aspects of how you want the load balancer to do its thing. Furthermore, you might not just setup the load balancer entirely in-advance, such that it is acting in a static manner during the load balancing, but instead might have the load balancer figuring out what action to take dynamically, in real-time.

When using load balancing for resiliency or redundancy purposes, there is a standard nomenclature of referring to the number of resources as N, and then appending a plus sign along with an integer value that ranges from 0 to some number M. If I say that my system is setup as N+0, I'm saying that there are zero or no redundancy devices. If I say it is N+1, then that implies there is 1 and only 1 such redundancy device. And so on.

You might be thinking that I should always have a plentiful set of redundancy devices, since that would seem the safest bet. But, there's a cost associated with the redundancy. Why was my stove top limited to just four burners? Because I wasn't willing to shell out the bigger bucks to get the model that had eight. I had assumed that for my cooking needs, the four sized stove was sufficient, and actually ample.

For computer systems, the same kind of consideration needs to come to play.

How many devices do I need and how much redundancy do I

need, which has to be considered in light of the costs involved. This can be a significant decision in that later on it can be harder and even costlier to adjust. In the case of my stove top, the kitchen was built in such a manner that the four burner sized stove top fits just right. If I were to now decide that I want the eight burner version, it's not just a simple plug-and-play, instead they would need to knock out my kitchen counters, and likely some of the flooring, and so on. The choice I made at the start has somewhat locked me in, though of course if I want to have the kids doing cooking more of the time, it might be worth the dough to expand the kitchen accordingly.

In computing, you can consider load balancing for just about anything. It might be the CPU processors that underlie your system. It could be the GPUs. It could be the servers. You can load balance on an actual hardware basis, and you can also do load balancing on a virtualized system. The target resource is often referred to as an endpoint, or perhaps a replica, or a device, or some other such wording.

Those in computing that don't explicitly consider the matter of load balancing are either unaware of the significance of it or are unsure of what it can achieve.

For many AI software developers, they figure that it's really a hardware issue or maybe an operating system issue, and thus they don't put much of their own attention toward the topic. Instead, they hope or assume that those OS specialists or hardware experts have done whatever is required to figure out any needed load balancing.

Similar to my example about my four burner stove, the problem with this kind of thinking is that if later on the AI application is not running at a suitable performance level and all of a sudden you want to do something about load balancing, the horse is already out of the barn. Just like my notion of possibly replacing the four burner stove with an eight burner, it can take a lot of effort and cost to retrofit for load balancing.

What does this have to do with AI self-driving cars?

At the Cybernetic AI Self-Driving Car Institute, we are developing AI systems for self-driving cars. One key aspect of an AI system for a self-driving car is its ability to perform responsively in real-time.

On-board of the self-driving car you have numerous processors that are intended to run the AI software. This can also include various GPUs and other specialized devices.

Per my overall framework of AI self-driving cars, here are some the key driving tasks involved:

- Sensor data collection and interpretation

- Sensor fusion

- Virtual world model updating

- AI action planning

- Car controls command issuance

You've got software that needs to run in real-time and direct the activities of a car. The car will at times be in motion. There will be circumstances wherein the AI is relatively at ease and there's not much happening, and there will be situations whereby the AI is having to work at a rip-roaring pace. Imagine going on a freeway at 75 miles per hour, and there's lots of other nearby traffic, along with foul weather, the road itself has potholes, there's debris on the roadway, and so on. A lot of things, all happening at once.

The AI holds in its automation the key to whether the self-driving car safely navigates and avoids getting into a car accident. This is not just a real-time system, it is a real-time system that can spell life and death. Human occupants in the AI self-driving car can get harmed if the AI can't operate in time to make the proper decision. Pedestrians can get harmed. Other cars can get hit, and thus the human occupants of those cars can get harmed. All in all, this is quite serious business.

To achieve this, the on-board hardware generally has lots of computing power and lots of redundancy. Is it enough? That's the zillion dollar question. Similar to my choice of a four burner stove, when the automotive engineers for the auto maker or tech firm decide to outfit the self-driving car with whatever number and type of processors and other such devices, they are making some hard choices about what the performance capability of that self-driving car will be. If the AI cannot run fast enough to make sound choices, it's a bad situation all around.

Imagine too that you are fielding your self-driving car. It seems to be running fine in the roadway trials underway. You give the green light to ramp up production of the self-driving car. These self-driving cars start to roll off the assembly line and the public at large is buying them.

Suppose after this has taken place for a while, you begin to get reports that there are times that the AI seemed to not perform in time. Maybe it even froze up. Not good.

Some self-driving car pundits say that it's easy to solve this. Via OTA (Over The Air) updates, you just beam down into the self-driving cars a patch for whatever issue or flaw there was in the AI software. I've mentioned many times that the use of OTA is handy, important, and significant, but it is not a cure all.

Let's suppose that the AI software has no bugs or errors in this case. Instead, it's that the AI running via the on-board processors is exhausting the computing power at certain times. Maybe this only happens once in a blue moon, but if you are depending upon your life and the life of others, even a once in a blue moon is too much of a problem. It could be that the computing power is just insufficient.

What do you do then? Yes, you can try to optimize the AI and get it to somehow not consume so much computing power. This though is harder than it seems. If you opt to toss more hardware at this problem, sure, that's' possible, but now this means that all of those AI self-driving cars that you sold will need to come back into the auto shop and get added hardware. Costly. Logistically arduous. A mess.

Some auto makers and tech firms find themselves confronting the classic silo mentality of the software side and the hardware side of their development groups. The software side developing the AI is not so concerned about the details of the hardware and just expect that their AI will run in proper time. The hardware side puts in place as much computing power as it seems can be suitably provided, depending on cost considerations, physical space considerations, etc.

If there is little or no load balancing that comes to play, in terms of making sure that both the software and hardware teams come together on how to load balance, it's a recipe for disaster.

Some might say that all they need to know is how much raw speed is needed, whether it is MIPS (millions of instructions per second), FLOPS (floating point operations per second), TPU's (tensor processing units), or other such metrics. This though doesn't fully answer the performance question. The AI software side often doesn't really know what kind of performance resources they'll need per se.

You can try to simulate the AI software to gauge how much performance it will require. You can create benchmarks. There are all sorts of "lab" kinds of ways to gauge usage. Once you've got AI self-driving cars in the field for trials, you should also be pulling stats about performance. Indeed, it's quite important that their be on-board monitoring to see how the AI and the hardware are performing.

With proper load balancing on-board the self-driving car, the load balancer is trying to keep the AI from getting starved, it is trying to ensure that the AI runs undisrupted by whatever might be happening at the hardware level. The load balance is monitoring the devices involved. When saturation approaches, this can be potentially handled via static or dynamic balancing, and thus the load balancer needs to come to play.

If an on-board device goes sour, the load balancer hopefully has a means to deal with the loss. Whether it's redundancy or whether it is shifting over to have another device now do double-duty, you've got to have a load balancer on-board to deal with those moments. And do so in real-time. While the self-driving car is possibly in motion, on a crowded freeway, etc.

Believe it or not, I've had some AI developers say to me that it is ridiculous to think that any of the on-board hardware devices are going to just up and quit. They cannot fathom any reason for this to occur.

I point out that the on-board devices are all prone to the same kinds of hardware failures as any piece of hardware. There's nothing magical about being included into a self-driving car. There will be "bad" devices that will go out much sooner than their life expectancy. There will be devices that will go out due to some kind of in-car issue that arises, maybe overheating or maybe somehow a human occupant manages to bust it up. There are bound to be recalls on some of that hardware.

Also, I've seen some of them deluded by the aspect that during the initial trials of self-driving cars, the auto maker or tech firm is pampering the AI self-driving car. After each journey or maybe at the end of the day, the tech team involved in the trials are testing to make sure that all of the hardware is still in pristine shape. They swap out equipment as needed. They act like a race car team, continually tuning and making sure that everything on-board is in top shape. There's nearly an unlimited budget of sorts during these trials in that the view is do whatever it takes to keep the AI self-driving car running.

This is not what's going to happen once the real-world occurs.

When those self-driving cars are being used by the average Joe or Samatha, they will not have a trained team of self-driving car specialists at the ready to tweak and replace whatever might need to be replaced. The equipment will age. It will suffer normal wear and tear. It will even be taxed beyond normal wear and tear since it is anticipated that AI self-driving cars will be running perhaps 24x7, nearly non-stop.

For those auto makers and tech firms that are giving short shrift right now to the importance of load balancing, I hope that this might be a wake-up call.

It's not going to do anyone any good, neither the public and nor the makers of AI self-driving cars, if it turns out that the AI is unable to get the performance it needs out of the on-board devices. A load balancer is not a silver bullet, but it at least provides the kind of added layer of protection that you'd expect for any solidly devised real-time system.

Presumably, there aren't any auto makers or tech firms that opted to go with the four burner stove when an eight burner stove was needed. Either way, just like my kids, you'll need some kind of algorithm or automation that will do the needed load balancing.

CHAPTER 7
VIRTUAL SPIKE STRIPS
AND
AI SELF-DRIVING CARS

CHAPTER 7

VIRTUAL SPIKE STRIPS
AND
AI SELF-DRIVING CARS

In many parking lots where you need to pay to get into the parking area, the exits often have a series of metal spikes that are pointed toward any cars that might be tempted to sneak into the lot. That small strip of spikes is enough to likely puncture the tires of any trespassing car that has a driver intent on avoiding paying any fees to use the parking lot. Cars that are properly exiting the parking lot are able to readily rollover the spikes since the spikes are angled away from that direction and usually on a spring action, so they suppress under the pressure of the car tires and the weight of the car.

I've never actually seen someone try to drive the wrong way over those metal spikes and it seems to be a pretty good deterrent. We all readily accept the idea that they are there for the purpose of preventing interlopers. They are handy too since those leaving the parking lot don't need to do anything special to get out. Unlike a gate arm that might need to lift up, those metal teeth just sit there, grimacing at those that want to tempt fate and see if they can somehow ride across their lethal smile.

There's another use for these metal teeth.

Here in Southern California, we are somewhat known as the capital of car chases for the United States. Some statistics claim that we average one car chase a day throughout the year. Our sunny weather probably helps encourage drivers to consider going on a car chase. Along with our apparent obsession with cars and wanting to drive cars.

The police usually catch the driver of the car that's leading the chase, but this fact doesn't seem to overly discourage people from launching into a car chase. When the person being chased has a long track record of lawbreaking and has committed some crime coinciding with the undertaking being pursued, such as robbing a liquor store, it makes relative sense that they might try to run, even if the odds of successfully getting away are relatively low. The chases that are especially peculiar involve the situations wherein the person fleeing has no criminal track record and the crime they committed such as rolling through a stop sign is not commensurate with the escalation into a car chase, and the legal troubles they'll get into for the chase are so severe it just belies logic that the person would take such rash action.

You might be aware that there is controversy about whether or not the police should even undertake such chases. A wild car chase through populated areas can be highly dangerous for everyone involved. The person that's being sought is often a desperate driver, willing to ram other cars, hit pedestrians, drive on sidewalks, drive the wrong way on the roads, and otherwise do anything to get away. Besides the police being endangered as they try to follow such illegal antics, there is the danger to bystanders and other innocents that had nothing to do with the matter other than being in the wrong place at the right time.

In some jurisdictions, the police will at times stay back from the frantic driver and try not to seemingly pressure the driver into doing the especially dangerous maneuvers. In some cases, the police follow by helicopter rather than by police car. There have been instances whereby the police let the person zoom along and get away, doing so because they knew that the person had a limited criminal record and also knew their identity and where they live. Some would argue it is a safer approach to the matter to call-off the chase and try to catch the person later on, rather than "provoke" them into a car chase mode and have something untoward occur. It's all debatable.

A recent car chase was one for the record books since the driver opted to go onto train tracks. This is a rather unusual attempt to get away. Furthermore, the driver then kept on the rails and went into an underground train tunnel. The driver was going the wrong way into the tunnel, which meant that a train would be coming in the other direction and could potentially smash head-on into the car. While watching the car chase unfold on TV, there were many that thought the driver was pretty stupid to go into the tunnel since the police could quickly place guards at either end and the driver would have no means of escape.

When the car did not pop-up by coming out of the other side of the tunnel, it began to dawn on people that perhaps the desperado was going to hide inside the tunnel. Turns out, the person abandoned the car and tried to come up to the street level via various of the tunnel escape hatches. The police caught them, doing so at the point of the escape hatches and for one of them at some distance from an escape hatch.

Some might wonder why the police need to undertake a car chase when presumably they can simply try to disable the car involved. Indeed, you've probably seen that the police often will try to lay down a strip of metal spikes in the hopes that the wayward driver will drive over the spikes. These traffic spikes are also sometimes called tire shredders. Other names for the spikes include being referred to as stop sticks, jack rocks, and stingers.

These strips function in the same way that the parking lot strips do. The notion is that a car will try to rollover the spikes, the spikes will puncture the tires, and the tires will either deflate or be torn apart. Without viable tires, in theory the car chase should come to an end. The driver would not be able to control the car without viable tires and would not be able to drive at high speeds without viable tires. Trying to continue driving would be difficult and the odds are that relatively soon the driver would be driving on the rims of the tires.

Again, as the apparent capital of car chases, I'll say that we have had quite a number of car chases that involves the driver still trying to drive the car, in spite of having had the tires punctured. One car chase involved the driver continuing for several miles, and sparks were flying as the rims were essentially acting as a tire. Eventually, the sparks ignited some other parts of the car, and the entire car became engulfed in flames. It was actually impressive how long the car itself withstood this treatment and was maybe a testament to the makers of the car that it was able to continue that long.

In any case, the metal barbs or spikes are supposed to either stop the car nearly dead in its tracks or at least cause enough damage that the car is not going to presumably be further drivable. In some cases, the teeth are made to detach. This is thought to be a further means of damaging the tire, since the detached teeth are intended to embed into the tire and continue causing damage. If a tire merely rolls across the teeth, there might or might not be deep damage done to the tire, but if the teeth themselves embed into the tire and stay with the tire, the thinking is that the metal spike will be able to do ongoing damage as long as the driver continues to drive the car.

You might find of interest that the teeth on a stop strip are often in the shape of a caltrop. For those of you that are history buffs, you might know that during the time of the Romans, caltrops were used to slow down horses during wars and possibly impact elephants and human troops. Essentially, a caltrop is a four toothed spike that when you throw it onto the ground there will be three teeth facing to the ground and one tooth facing up. In the case of horses, the notion was that a horse might step into the upward facing spike and injure the horse or at least frighten it into panic.

Perhaps it is remarkable that in this day and age, we still use the same kind of mechanism, doing so when trying to prevent cars from going improperly into a parking lot or when trying to stop a getaway car. Those Romans, they certainly were clever and had some long-lasting inventions (well, one cannot give them all the credit, there were others that had used caltrops even before them!).

What does this have to do with AI self-driving cars?

At the Cybernetic AI Self-Driving Car Institute, we are developing AI software for self-driving cars. One aspect that is a rather "thorny" topic, so to speak, involves the matter of externally stopping an AI self-driving car.

Allow me to elaborate.

First, let's clarify that there are varying levels of AI self-driving cars. The topmost level is considered Level 5. A Level 5 self-driving car is one that is being driven by the AI and there is no human driver involved. For the design of Level 5 self-driving cars, the auto makers are even removing the gas pedal, brake pedal, and steering wheel, since those are contraptions used by human drivers. The Level 5 self-driving car is not being driven by a human and nor is there an expectation that a human driver will be present in the self-driving car. It's all on the shoulders of the AI to drive the car.

For self-driving cars less than a Level 5, there must be a human driver present in the car. The human driver is currently considered the responsible party for the acts of the car. The AI and the human driver are co-sharing the driving task. In spite of this co-sharing, the human is supposed to remain fully immersed into the driving task and be ready at all times to perform the driving task. I've repeatedly warned about the dangers of this co-sharing arrangement and predicted it will produce many untoward results.

Let's consider two separate overall use cases, one involving a Level 5 self-driving car, which as I've mentioned would be a self-driving car being driven entirely and only by the AI, and the other case would be a less than Level 5 self-driving car for which there is a co-sharing of the human driver and the AI.

In a Level 5 self-driving car, there will be some form of conversational dialogue between the AI and the human occupants that involves the humans making requests of the AI that's driving the car. You get into a Level 5 self-driving car and tell it you want to be driven to the baseball stadium. The AI proceeds accordingly. Perhaps during the driving journey, you tell the AI to stop at the Starbucks that's down the street, so you can use their drive-thru to get some coffee before you get to the ballgame. And so on.

What kind of latitude do you have as the human directing the AI self-driving car?

Can you tell it to drive illegally? Maybe you are late getting to work one day, and so you tell the AI to exceed the posted speed limit on the highway that you take to get to work. The posted speed is 45 miles per hour, but you tell the AI to go 55 miles per hour, in hopes of getting to work on time. Should the AI obey such a command?

I'm betting that you are tempted to say that no, the AI should not obey a commend to undertake an illegal driving act. Your wanting to get to work on-time is not much of a reason to have the AI perform an illegal driving action and also it could be dangerous too since the rest of the traffic might be going 45 mph and meanwhile the AI self-driving car might be swerving around other cars to go the desired 55 mph. Could be unsafe and produce a car crash of some kind.

But, maybe you are in the Level 5 self-driving car and you are bleeding profusely because you somehow had gotten cut, or maybe someone is in the self-driving car that is pregnant and about to deliver a baby, under those circumstances would it make sense to allow the AI to go ahead at 55 mph rather than 45 mph, even though it would be an illegal driving act? I'm assuming you are more sympathetic in such instances to allowing the AI to "break the law" as part of its driving efforts.

The point being that we as a society have yet to wrestle with the range of legal and "illegal" acts of what an AI of a self-driving car is going to be "allowed" to do in terms of the driving task. It's going to be a crucial matter once we start to see the advent of AI self-driving cars on our roadways.

So far, I think you can see that there's going to be a fine line between the strict legal kind of driving that we assume an AI self-driving car will do and the potential need for the AI to be permitted to go beyond the normally stated constraints.

Let's consider the car chase predicament.

If you were to tell your AI self-driving car to proceed to lead a car chase, telling it to go at very high speeds and try to be evasive as it drives, should it do so?

I'm sure you are saying that even the suggestion that the AI would abide by such a command is absurd on the face of things. Have an AI self-driving car that starts a car chase? Nuts! This should never happen.

Suppose that you have just survived a potential carjacking and are desperate to get away from attackers that are trying to get you. Maybe you are a celebrity or a very wealthy person that is being sought by some bad people. Maybe it's a gang that just wanted to get your wallet and your car. Indeed, in terms of cars, there are some that believe we'll begin to see "robojacking" of AI self-driving cars, an obviously undesirable trend that might arise as self-driving cars become more prevalent.

Would it be OK then for the AI self-driving car in this instance be able to proceed as though being car chased and therefore be at the forefront of the car chase? I'm guessing you are now more sympathetic to the notion. Sure, if an innocent person's life might depend on it, maybe having the AI proceed to try and getaway makes sense.

If the AI was trying to do a getaway because the person had committed an illegal act, such as robbing a bank, I'm sure we would all agree this kind of a car chase effort should not be condoned. Or, maybe the human is drunk and blurts out to the AI that it should start driving evasively because Martians are on the way to beam them up to Mars. This is another circumstance that I believe we would all agree is not warranted for the AI to take such rash driving tactics.

For the moment, can we agree that there might be valid cases of the AI undertaking evasive driving action for which we could construe the driving to be the rudiments of a car chase? The AI would be driving the car at a fast pace, attempting to allude followers, and likely would be committing "illegal" driving efforts as it does so.

121

If you agree with that aforementioned notion, we then need to figure out how far are we willing to have the AI go on this matter.

Can the AI drive the self-driving car on the wrong side of the street? Can it drive on sidewalks? Can it swerve around other cars? These are all dangerous acts that could potentially harm others.

Here's your conundrum. If you say that the AI cannot do any kind of driving that might harm others, I challenge you to then explain what exactly the AI can do during this evasive driving? It's not much of an evasive driving if the self-driving car is driving along just as a normal car does, and I'd dare say that's not evasive driving at all.

You might try to suggest that the AI needs to be astute enough to ferret out a legitimate request for driving evasively and those that are not legitimate. If the car was being driven by a human chauffer, we would likely expect that human to be able to discern between a person that gets into the car and has just robbed a bank versus someone that gets into the car and is about to deliver a baby.

This logic though doesn't especially do us much good since even if the human chauffer realized that the person had just robbed a bank, and suppose the chauffer then refused to drive evasively, the bank robber might point a gun at the chauffer and say drive evasively anyway. The chauffer has to then make a choice between presumably staying alive and driving evasively, versus refusing to do so and possibly getting shot and killed. Maybe I've seen too many movies, but I think most humans would opt to drive evasively and hope that somehow, they will otherwise be able to escape the situation.

The point here is that the AI is unlikely to be able to ferret out the matter of whether driving evasively is warranted or not. Maybe far in the future when someday there is AI that is more akin to the "singularity" that some speak of, but for now, the common sense reasoning of the AI is quite limited and there's not much likelihood we'll see it become so advanced that it can be available for the advent of AI self-driving cars (though, some AI pundits say that only via breakthroughs in common sense reasoning for AI will we even achieve true Level 5 self-driving cars).

At this juncture of the discussion, I hope you are at least open to the notion that we might end-up with AI self-driving cars that are driving evasively, doing so with a presumed purpose, whether or not the purpose is considered legitimate by society or not.

Though the focus herein involves an AI self-driving car that is seemingly driving at a fast clip and doing dangerous driving tactics, I'll point out that my next comments herein could even apply to a situation of an AI self-driving car that appears to be driving in a perfectly normal everyday way. Please keep that in mind.

Suppose that an AI self-driving car is driving in a manner that we otherwise don't want it to do be doing so, and we want to essentially stop the self-driving car.

How could that be accomplished?

You could use those metal spike strips. In other words, regardless of whether we are trying to stop a human driven car or an AI self-driving car of a Level 5, the use of the tire shredders could still be invoked.

Toss those strips in front of an oncoming Level 5 self-driving car. What happens? Assuming that the AI is not able to avoid rolling over the metal teeth, the tires would presumably get punctured. At this point, the AI is now continuing to try and drive the self-driving car. Doing so is rough at this juncture. The self-driving car is going to lurch and have the same difficulties that any normal car would have when the tires have been punctured.

Few of the auto makers and tech firms are working on how to have the AI deal with circumstances such as having the tires shredded and still be able to safely drive the car. They consider this kind of problem to be an "edge" problem. An edge problem is one that is at the periphery of the core problem that you are trying to solve. At this time, the AI developers are primarily concerned about getting an AI self-driving car to drive along properly on a properly working self-driving car on a properly devised roadway in properly good weather. That's considered core.

Do we need the AI to ultimately be able to deal with other problems associated with the physical aspects of the self-driving car? Absolutely. A self-driving car is like any other car in that it will have physical breakdowns and problems. A human driver would need to accommodate such difficulties, and so should the AI. We cannot assume that all self-driving cars will always work just dandy, which for the roadway trials taking place now is pretty much the assumption. Today's AI self-driving cars are being pampered, but once they get into the real-world and no longer have a dedicated car pit crew, it will be a different story.

Besides the usual physical ways to stop a car, which would seem to apply to an AI self-driving car too, would we possibly have other means to try and stop an AI self-driving car?

Perhaps we might use a virtual spike strip.

By this, I mean that we could somehow convince the AI that it should bring the AI self-driving car to a stop.

We could possibly do so then without necessarily tossing a physical metal strip of spikes in front of the self-driving car. In lieu of that rather more blunt approach, we could make the AI bring the self-driving car to a halt simply because we told it to do so. In a sense, it is like a virtual kind of spike strip.

Presumably, this would be a lot safer too than a physical spike strip. The self-driving car is still intact and thus rather than shredding the tires and hoping that the self-driving car doesn't do a barrel roll and injure anyone including bystanders, the AI could presumably bring the self-driving car to a safe halt instead. Imagine how much safer this is for the police as well, wherein with physical strips they need to take a heightened risk of getting front of the car and deploy the strips (not as easy as it seems in the movies).

As an aside, we can consider even having the AI self-driving car take some other action, such as some have suggested that we could instruct an AI self-driving car being used as a getaway vehicle by criminals that that just robbed a bank and we might instruct the AI to bring them to the nearest police station. Wouldn't it be nice that the AI could wrap up those dastards in a nice tight bow and deliver them directly to the police? Well, I have my doubts about the practical nature of this suggestion, but that's something I'll tackle for you another day.

Let's then pursue the notion that we, whomever the "we" is, might commandeer the AI of the AI self-driving car and have the AI do something other than what perhaps the human occupants have told the AI to do.

How could we control the AI in this manner, doing so externally of the AI self-driving car?

One somewhat obvious way might be to use the OTA (Over The Air) capability of the AI self-driving car. The OTA is normally used to get data from the self-driving car, such as sensory data, and also provide updates to the self-driving car. When a new version of the AI software is needed for your AI self-driving car, it via OTA can connect to the cloud setup by the auto maker or tech firm, and receive those updates sent via electronic communication. No need to take your car into the auto shop for such updates.

Suppose the police see an AI self-driving car that is rocketing down the freeway, presumably being chased or potentially a car that the police will want to chase. The police might instead make contact with the auto maker or tech firm that setup the cloud OTA for this particular brand of AI self-driving car and have the auto maker or tech firm presumably send an electronic command to the self-driving car that instructs the self-driving car to come an immediate safe stop.

Lest you think this might take a long time to do, it could be all orchestrated beforehand. The police might already have a ready means to send such a request to an auto maker or tech firm. Perhaps entering the license plate number of the self-driving car into a special app by the police department and then the rest happens as fast as any usual electronic communication can do so. The auto maker or tech firm might not have any human intervention involved and just assume that any bona fide electronic command to tell an AI self-driving car that's using the OTA will then automatically send out such a command. Could happen in seconds.

Problem solved! Or, should I say, problem solved?

You can imagine that this raises all sorts of societal entanglements. Should just any police officer be able to issue such a command, doing so at any time? That seems a bit Big Brother like. Suppose too that someone somehow got ahold of the police capability and they opted to use it for their own devious purposes? Furthermore, there's now a chance of a security breech that if you could hack this system then you might be able to stop an AI self-driving car. Maybe you could stop thousands of them all at once.

We're also somewhat overlooking the technological aspect that suppose the OTA is not able to send a signal to the AI self-driving car, perhaps the self-driving car is not in an area where it has connectivity. Or, maybe the OTA was disabled by the human using the self-driving car, intentionally doing so, either by sabotaging it or maybe putting some kind of dampening mechanism to prevent the OTA from functioning.

Another approach might be to have the police physically display something that the AI self-driving car would "see" and therefore invoke the halt command in that manner. This is handy since it does not rely on any electronic communication over the airwaves. Forget about the OTA, and instead just physically present something to the attention of the AI self-driving car. This presumes that you are physically near to the AI self-driving car, which of course if you were using actual metal strips you would need to be anyway.

Keeping in mind that the AI self-driving car has cameras for visual processing of the surroundings, you might have agreed beforehand with the auto maker or tech firm that if a certain kind of image is seen by the sensors, the AI self-driving car will come to an immediate safe halt. Thus, the police arrange to get in front of where the AI self-driving car is driving toward, and they hold-up a sign that has this special image on it (actually, since there are cameras pointing to the rear of the car too, the police could do this from behind the self-driving car and don't even need to try and get in front of it; that's a "nice" difference in comparison to actual physical metal strips wherein you need to get in front of a speeding car!).

Here's the usual steps involved in the AI driving task:

- Sensor data collection and interpretation
- Sensor fusion
- Virtual world model updating
- AI action planning
- Car controls command issuance

Let's assume then that the police hold-up the special image, the camera sensors detect the image, and during the sensor data collection and interpretation the AI system realizes it is indeed the special image. The virtual world model which is being used to keep track of the surroundings of where the AI self-driving car is driving, the model is then used by the AI to try and identify a safe place to come to an immediate halt. Maybe it determines that up ahead a quarter mile would be the safest spot and allow for a gradual reduction in speed rather than slamming on the brakes. The AI action planning routine then devises the driving tasks to do so and sends those commands to the car controls.

Voila, the AI self-driving car now comes to a safe halt.

I mentioned that the sign might be a special visual image. Since most AI self-driving cars also have radar sensors, sonic sensors, and LIDAR, we don't necessarily need to even use a physical visual sign. It could be something else that might trigger the same kind of response. Perhaps an electronic signal might be used. Or a shape of some kind that might be detected by the radar. Or, there might be triggers established beforehand for each of the various sensors, thus, increasing the odds that the AI self-driving car will one way or another be able to detect the command.

One advantage of this approach would be that there's no need to rely upon an electronic communication that is remotely being beamed to the AI self-driving car. Instead, if you are within physical proximity, you can trigger it to abide by the signal. The odds are that the sensors of the AI self-driving car are going to be working, since otherwise the AI self-driving car is generally not going to be able to be driven anyway. It relies upon those sensors to be able to detect the environment and drive the car accordingly.

We're once again though finding ourselves facing the issue of who can rightfully make use of these special images or signals? Can any police or authority do so? Suppose it gets leaked out how these triggers work, and someone opts to use them for devious purposes. And so on.

You might also find of interest that there have already been some efforts undertaken to demonstrate that you can potentially fool a Machine Learning algorithm by doing something like this. Suppose you've used Machine Learning to train toward detecting stops signs. A sneaky means has been shown possible to train that Machine Learning to potentially ignore the stop sign if there's a certain image on the stop sign, like a simple yellow post-it note.

On this overall topic, there are some AI developers that are worried that even having a special program or routine embedded in the AI system that can be triggered and would bring the AI self-driving car to a halt is itself a dangerous "hole" in their view. In essence, once such a routine or program exists within the AI that's on-board the AI self-driving car, it means that one way or another it can somehow potentially be invoked. This could be done by someone that is considered authorized to do so, or by someone that is not authorized to do so (or, one supposes it could even be accidentally invoked by the AI itself, and unexpectedly and erratically come to a halt for no apparent sensible reason).

Some would argue that the AI should not have a specific routine or program for this purpose per se, and instead would merely take as input the "suggestion" of coming to an immediate safe halt. In essence, the communication to the AI self-driving car, whether electronic or via visual image or whatever, is not so much a command as it is a request. Someone or something is making a request of the AI, and the AI would need to decide whether or not to comply with the request.

This might even involve the AI asking the human occupants whether or not they want the AI to bring the self-driving car to a safe halt. It might be that the AI tells them that a request has been issued to do so, and it wants to hear their side of the story. They might tell the AI, yes, please go ahead and bring the AI self-driving car to a safe halt. Probably, and much more likely, they would tell the AI to ignore the request. In which case, what does the AI do then?

Admittedly, using physical metal strips to stop a car are a bit more straightforward. Most of the time, those strips are only in the possession of the police. Most of the time, they are only using the strips when the circumstances seem generally to merit it. This is usually done in the public view. Everyone can see that it is taking place. The virtual spike strips, which can be done "in secret" seem to raise all sorts of other thorny questions, as I had so suggested was the case earlier in this discussion.

You might note that I have not covered so far in this discussion the question about what to do when the AI is a less than Level 5 self-driving car.

I'll leave it to you to ponder this, but the mainstay of the issue would be whether the AI in a co-sharing driving task should be able to exert control over the self-driving car such that even if the human driver does not want to come to a halt, the AI would force it to happen anyway. As food for thought, if we are going to say that the human driver of an AI self-driving car for less than a Level 5 is considered the responsible driver, and yet we are willing to have the AI completely take over control of the self-driving car, this seems to open a can of worms.

We are also making an assumption throughout all of this discussion that the AI would readily be able to bring the AI self-driving car to an "immediate" and "safe" halt.

What timeframe constitutes the word immediate? Within seconds, minutes, or how long is permitted to execute the halt? In terms of "safe" that's also a somewhat tenuous notion. In a utopian world, sure, the AI might be able ensure a completely safe stop. In the real-world, suppose the AI pulls to the side of the freeway, and meanwhile a car that was behind the self-driving car gets confused and rams into the back of the self-driving car, killing the occupants. Was that a safe means to stop the car?

Right now, most of this kind of discussion is not yet taking place overtly. As mentioned, it is generally considered an edge problem for now.

Once we have prevalent AI self-driving cars, the topic will become more mainstream. Do we need some kind of virtual spike strips for AI self-driving cars? If so, what would it consist of? How would it be used? These are other such questions are not just technological, but also societal aspects that will need some very thought-provoking consideration. In the meantime, please do watch out for those metal strips!

CHAPTER 8
RAZZLE DAZZLE
CAMOUFLAGE
AND
AI SELF-DRIVING CARS

CHAPTER 8

RAZZLE DAZZLE CAMOUFLAGE
AND
AI SELF-DRIVING CARS

We generally think of camouflage as a means to blend into the surroundings. Many animals have a colorization pattern that allows them to seemingly disappear by laying quietly at a standstill on a tree branch or hiding inside a bush. Military personnel often put on special camouflage designated clothing and use skin paints to try and likewise be indistinguishable from their surroundings. The hope is that the enemy cannot spot them and so would be unable to accurately aim at them for purposes of attack.

This overall notion of camouflage is just one of several classes of camouflage, in this case the attempt at concealment is referred to as a crypsis form of camouflage.

There's another form of camouflage that we don't often consider, namely the kind that is known as motion dazzle, also sometimes called razzle dazzle, or perhaps more easily understood by the name disruptive camouflage. In this instance, the desire is to actually standout and be readily seen. In fact, being seen is the part that involves the camouflage trickery, specifically that the use of colors and shapes makes the observer take notice. In addition, the use of disruptive patterns and even countershading make it difficult for the observer to readily figure out the true shape and nature of what is being camouflaged.

This idea of using disruptive camouflage was extensively undertaken during World War I and also somewhat during World War II.

We tend to think of navy ships as always being painted a rather dull monotone grey color. This would seem to be a wise choice. At sea, the navy ships would tend to blend into the background of a greyish sky and a blue sea. Presumably, whales and dolphins use a similar colorization to try and blend into their surroundings. Here in Southern California, you can wander to San Diego and see lots of United States Navy ships docked in the harbor as it is a major west coast naval center. Many visitors often say to me that they didn't even notice the big ships, in spite of the fact that there are many dozens of them all readily seen. Must be the grey monotone.

In a controversial manner, upon the onset of World War I, there were some that suggested it would be better to use a disruptive camouflage pattern for navy ships rather than a monotone grey. Various complex patterns involving striking geometric shapes were devised and painted onto navy ships of the time period. Thousands of such motion dazzle depictions were used. The colors and shapes are intersecting of each other and interrupting of each other. It was said that Picasso himself found these ship colorizations to be inspiring.

Why would anyone in their right mind do this to navy ships? Isn't it just asking for those ships to be readily attacked by submarines, airplanes, and other enemy ships? Wouldn't it be better to try to hide or conceal the ships so that the enemy would not realize it is floating along on the sea? There indeed were acrimonious debates on this topic.

Those that favored the disruptive camouflage claimed that the navy ships were inevitably going to be spotted anyway and that trying to hide or conceal them was generally ineffective. If you are in agreement that the concealment approach is not going to be successful, then you would certainly be open to considering other options. The razzle dazzle approach was intended to not only make the ships seen but that when seen it would be potentially confusing to the enemy as to what they were looking at.

An enemy might not be sure if the ship is a battleship or a destroyer. It would be hard to discern the type of ship and also whether the ship was heading toward you or away from you. The speed was not easy to estimate either. Are you looking at the bow or the stern of the ship? All of this disruptive kind of visualization was intended to confound the enemy. Since it was assumed that the enemy was likely going to spot the ships anyway, might as well try and make things hard for the enemy to figure out what the ship was and where it was going.

Those navies that adopted the razzle dazzle were also smart enough to realize that if they painted certain kinds of ships the same way, such as all battleships in the same patterns and colors, it would undermine the purpose of the disruptive notion. It would mean that once the enemy figured out how you were discoloring that category of ships, they could easily then "break the code" and be able to figure out what kind of ship it was and how to interpret the colors and patterns. As such, those using the razzle dazzle had to come up with varying patterns and use them in a somewhat unique manner for each individual ship.

There are zoological theories that suggest the zebra, jaguar, and giraffe are examples of a razzle dazzle form of camouflage. There is much contention whether those animals are indeed going the razzle dazzle route or whether there is some other reason for the patterns and colors on their skins. For example, some say that the giraffe is actually attempting to use the traditional form of camouflage by having the colors that you might see associated with trees. Given that giraffes stand tall, maybe the idea is that nature led them toward concealment when among a clump of trees.

In terms of the navy use of disruptive camouflage, numerous scientific studies have tried to determine whether or not the razzle dazzle is really more effective than the monotone grey. It would seem that most studies ultimately are unable to control sufficiently the numerous factors involved and it is a muddied picture as to whether the razzle dazzle is truly an effective defensive technique. There are some that say it is a freakish method and all it does is make the ships look like bizarre oddities.

What does this have to do with AI self-driving cars?

At the Cybernetic AI Self-Driving Car Institute, we are developing AI software for self-driving cars. One aspect that is going to be crucial for the ultimate success of self-driving cars will be whether pedestrians are safe when around AI self-driving cars.

Allow me to elaborate.

First, let's clarify that there are varying levels of AI self-driving cars. The topmost level is considered Level 5. A Level 5 self-driving car is one that is being driven by the AI and there is no human driver involved. For the design of Level 5 self-driving cars, the auto makers are even removing the gas pedal, brake pedal, and steering wheel, since those are contraptions used by human drivers. The Level 5 self-driving car is not being driven by a human and nor is there an expectation that a human driver will be present in the self-driving car. It's all on the shoulders of the AI to drive the car.

For self-driving cars less than a Level 5, there must be a human driver present in the car. The human driver is currently considered the responsible party for the acts of the car. The AI and the human driver are co-sharing the driving task. In spite of this co-sharing, the human is supposed to remain fully immersed into the driving task and be ready at all times to perform the driving task. I've repeatedly warned about the dangers of this co-sharing arrangement and predicted it will produce many untoward results.

Let's focus herein on the true Level 5 self-driving car. Much of the comments apply to the less than Level 5 self-driving cars too, but the fully autonomous AI self-driving car will receive the most attention in this discussion.

One of the top worries that the auto makers and tech firms have about AI self-driving cars will be the interaction of AI self-driving cars and pedestrians.

In theory, the AI self-driving car is supposed to be good enough at the driving task to be able to detect pedestrians. Once so detected, the AI should be doing what it can to avoid hitting pedestrians. There are some pundits that keep referring to "zero fatalities" once AI self-driving cars have been adopted on a widespread basis, but I've said many times that this zero-fatality notion is nonsensical.

Imagine that an AI self-driving car is driving down a street at the legally posted speed. Suppose it is 45 miles per hour, which is about 66 feet per second. A pedestrian is standing behind a pole that is adjacent to the road and right at the curb. Neither an AI self-driving car sees the pedestrian, and nor could a human driven car see the person that's standing behind that pole. The pedestrian decides to step out into the street just as the AI self-driving car gets within a few feet of the pole (or, if you like, pretend it was a human driver – the same end result is going to occur).

By what magic is the AI self-driving car not going to hit that pedestrian?

I ask the question because the answer is rather plain and simple, the law of physics is going to take over and the AI self-driving car is going to ram into that pedestrian. There was insufficient time to swerve the self-driving car. There was insufficient time to brake the self-driving car. There was no means to detect the pedestrian's presence beforehand. Wham. It happened. That's more than zero fatalities.

Well, I realize that you might object and say that it is preposterous that the pedestrian was unable to be seen. Maybe I've contrived the situation in a manner that could never happen.

I'm not sure where you drive, but I assure you that in the downtown Los Angeles area that I drive, it happens all the time that pedestrians are obscured from view. One time, a Fedex worker had stacked a bunch of boxes next to the curb, standing high about eight feet or so. Two pedestrians suddenly emerged from behind those boxes and stepped directly into the street. There was no viable means to have detected them beforehand.

Some of you might say that if they were jaywalking, it's their fault for having illegally attempted to cross the street. I'm not particularly discussing fault right now, and just trying to clarify and emphasize that pedestrians can mix with cars in a deadly fashion, and that an AI self-driving car is not necessarily going to somehow remedy entirely that equation.

If you still aren't convinced, and still believe that the "hidden" pedestrian is a falsehood, I'll change the indication and say that the pedestrian was completely seen by the car driver, whether it's a human driver or an AI self-driving car. Suppose the pedestrian is completely visible and there's no chance of not seeing the pedestrian.

Once again, if the pedestrian suddenly steps off the curb into the street, and if a car is approaching at 66 feet per second, and if the pedestrian does get in front of the car with just a second or two before impact, the law of physics enters into the picture. There will not be enough time to swerve the car or stop the car. It's going to hit the pedestrian.

Why would a pedestrian do this? Is it a suicide by car? No (well, I hope not). There are pedestrians that routinely step into the street and aren't at all paying attention to the cars. One recent concern by many municipalities if that people seem to be looking at their smartphones rather than the street traffic, and end-up making dumb moves into oncoming traffic. There are some local ordinances that have now made it against the law for you to be looking at your cell phone while crossing the street, even while doing so in a legal crosswalk.

In short, either a human driven car or an AI self-driving car can end-up hitting and possibly killing a pedestrian, doing so for sure in the circumstance wherein the pedestrian opts to enter into the street when there is no viable means of avoiding the pedestrian, neither by braking or swerving the car.

You might be thinking that shouldn't the AI self-driving car do a better job on this than a human driven car?

I suppose you could say that an AI self-driving car might do a better job in that the AI is presumably not distracted as a human driver might get distracted. A human driver might be looking at the other side of the street and noticing a new barbershop that's opened up, and thus fail to notice the pedestrian to their right that suddenly steps into the street.

If there is a chance to avoid striking the pedestrian, by-and-large you might say that the AI will perhaps be more likely to do so, since it lacks the distraction factor that could bely a human driver. The AI is presumably continually scanning the surroundings, on all sides, and not going to allow itself to become preoccupied with one particular thing, such as the new barbershop.

Here's the usual steps involved in the AI driving task:

- Sensor data collection and interpretation
- Sensor fusion
- Virtual world model updating
- AI action planning
- Car controls command issuance

The AI self-driving car should be using all of its sensors, including cameras for visual images, radar, sonic, and LIDAR, trying to detect where pedestrians are. It's not sufficient though to just detect them, since you also need to try and predict what the pedestrian is going to do.

If a pedestrian is on the sidewalk and running, and they are veering toward the street, the AI is intended to make a prediction that the pedestrian might logically end-up in the street, and if intersecting with the path of the self-driving car, the AI should direct the AI self-driving car to avoid striking the pedestrian, once they (possibly) enter into the street.

Please keep in mind that the AI and the self-driving car are not considered perfect machines. Is there a chance that a pedestrian might not be detected in spite of the array of sensors on the self-driving car?

Yes, absolutely. Can the sensors themselves at times fail or falter? Yes, absolutely. Could the AI system end-up making a wrong choice about whether there is a pedestrian nearby and whether the pedestrian might be intending to get into harm's way? Yes, absolutely.

I say this because there are some pundits that seem to want to portray a utopian world that involves self-driving cars that are always working and always flawless. I ask you, can you cite for me any of today's machines that are utterly perfect and always flawless? I don't think so. The self-driving car is still a car. It is prone to equipment wear-and-tear. There might even be parts on the self-driving car that are subject to a recall. The AI itself might have bugs or errors in the software. And so on.

Let's then assume that the AI self-driving car is going to do what it can to avoid hitting pedestrians, but that it is not a perfect system and there are still substantive chances of hitting pedestrians, especially when a pedestrian does something erratic or rash.

There are some AI developers that say we should go after the pedestrians. In other words, if we cannot make the AI good enough to deal with the pedestrians, let's change the behavior of pedestrians. It's those pesky humans that are the real problem here. The AI is fine if it is just good enough, and we can presumably bend the will of humans so that the AI won't get itself into trouble.

I'm not one that ascribes to this notion that the pedestrians are the entire problem per se, and I'm a strong advocate that we need to make the AI stronger and self-driving cars more robust to be able to contend with pedestrians.

Nonetheless, admittedly the behavior of pedestrians does enter into the matter at-hand. That being said, trying to change human behavior is not an easy thing. I dare say that the jurisdictions that have outlawed looking at your cell phone as you cross the street are finding that most pedestrians are still looking down at their cell phones. Unless you were to put police at those crosswalks and they write a zillion tickets, few pedestrians are going to heed the new law.

There are though some aspects about human behavior that we can try to contend with.

One aspect is to try and grab the attention of the pedestrian so that they are less likely to blindly step into the path of an AI self-driving car.

At my presentations about AI self-driving cars, I've often described a phenomenon that I refer to as the "head nod" problem. For human driven cars, a pedestrian can usually see the human that is driving a car. There is usually a kind of "courtship" that takes place between a car driver and a pedestrian. The pedestrian might make eye contact and be subliminally saying that they are going to step out into the street and the car driver better let them do so. The car driver might be making eye contact to say that don't dare get in front of this car. In some cities, this takes place in a mere few seconds or so, such as in New York City or Boston, and a stare down leads to someone "winning" the chicken contest.

When you have an AI self-driving car, there is no longer a visually present human driver that represents the intentions of the self-driving car. Thus, an important signaling aspect of car-to-pedestrian is now removed from the day-to-day arrangement that we all seem to have with traffic and crossing streets or entering into streets. There's been an unwritten contract of sorts that pedestrians generally should look toward the driver and the driver should look toward pedestrians. It's not a perfect contract by any means. Pedestrians routinely don't look at a driver, or perhaps cannot see the driver anyway due to tinted windows or other obscurities.

We've been instituting various means of using conspicuity, already integral to the everyday capabilities of cars, doing so as a means for the AI to try and signal to pedestrians. Just like conventional cars, an AI self-driving car has its turn signals, its headlights, and can potentially use its horn too. Even the direction of the tires and the maneuvering of the physical motions of the car are all part of the signaling aspects to pedestrians.

More recently, there are some auto makers and tech firms that are making use of add-ons to an AI self-driving car to provide further signaling or messaging to pedestrians. These are pretty much experiments right now. No one is quite sure what kind of signaling or messaging might be best. Do you place an electronic signboard on the roof of the AI self-driving car? Do you put special wing like attachments on the sides of the AI self-driving car that can display visual signals? Do you include audio sounds, beyond just honking a horn, such as a tone to indicate when the AI self-driving car is making a turn, or even an automated Alexa or Siri like voice that says what the self-driving car is going to do?

There is also a move afoot to provide a V2P capability (vehicle to pedestrians).

There are already efforts toward V2V (vehicle to vehicle) communications, allowing an AI self-driving car to electronically communicate with another AI self-driving car. In a crowded downtown area, the AI self-driving car ahead of your AI self-driving car might via V2V warn your AI self-driving car that a pedestrian is about to step into the street.

And there are V2I efforts (vehicle to infrastructure) too, in which the roadway infrastructure such as street lights or even crosswalks will communicate electronically with your AI self-driving car.

The V2P is the idea that a pedestrian might have a smartphone or maybe a smartwatch (or other wearable), and the AI self-driving car could communicate with the pedestrian. This is kind of "head nod" aspect that I mentioned earlier, except taken into a modern day with the use of electronics. The AI self-driving car might broadcast to the pedestrians on the corner that the AI is intending to make a right turn on red when it reaches the intersection. This could forewarn the pedestrians.

Presumably, a pedestrian could also make a request to an AI self-driving car. Perhaps the pedestrian needs extra time to make it through the crosswalk, and so their electronic device sends an indication to an

AI self-driving car that's coming down the street. The AI then realizes that there might be a longer wait then normal up ahead at the crosswalk and would slow down or come to a stop accordingly.

I now present to you a somewhat provocative notion.

Should an AI self-driving car be readily noticed as an AI self-driving car?

Some would say that yes, it is important for pedestrians to realize that an AI self-driving car is coming along on the street. If they realize it is an AI self-driving car, perhaps the pedestrians will be more cautious than they otherwise might be. This could be especially important if we are conceding that in many respects the AI self-driving car might not be as good as a human driver in terms of dealing with pedestrians. By realizing that there is an AI self-driving car, the pedestrians are essentially forewarned.

So far, most of the AI self-driving cars tend to have a LIDAR unit on the top of the car, which is a beacon looking device. This is there for functional purposes. It also though happens to help make an AI self-driving car standout as an AI self-driving car. Visually, when you see the cap on the top of the self-driving car, you are likely looking at an AI self-driving car. Many in the general public already have become accustomed to this feature and immediately assume that any car with the beacon or cone is most likely an AI self-driving car.

Please be aware though that not all of the AI self-driving cars will necessarily opt to use LIDAR. Also, as the LIDAR units get improved and further miniaturized, it will become less obvious that there's a LIDAR unit on the top of some AI self-driving cars since they will be streamlined in shape and size.

Some might argue that we should purposely put a special kind of dome or cap on all AI self-driving cars, regardless of whether LIDAR is being used or not. Doing so would make it a visually obvious aspect that the car is an AI self-driving car. It might even be a regulated requirement that all AI self-driving cars would have to have one. It is mandated as kind of "decorative" matter (serving as a physical shape for distinctiveness, a footprint as it were), rather than for an electronic functional purpose.

And this brings us to the topic of razzle dazzle!

Right now, most of the auto makers and tech firms are taking a conventional looking car and outfitting it to be an AI self-driving car. The shape and colorization of the AI self-driving car is pretty much the same as any other car on the roadways today. There are some future concept cars that have designs of a rather new look, but those aren't particularly aimed to be on our roadways soon.

Maybe, if we extend the idea of having a dome or beacon on the top of an AI self-driving car, we might consider doing something even more extravagant about the shape and colors of an AI self-driving car.

We already accept the notion that a cab or taxi is often yellow in color and has an indicator on the roof. We accept the notion that police cars have a certain pattern and color scheme. Would it make sense to consider that all AI self-driving cars would need to abide by some special designated "razzle dazzle" combination of shapes and colors?

The rather obvious downside to this idea is that perhaps the public might not like the razzle dazzle look. If you are an auto maker pouring tons of money into AI self-driving cars, you probably don't want to risk having people not be willing to buy an AI self-driving car because of how it looks. Remember before that some expressed that the razzle dazzle looking navy ships are freakish in appearance? I doubt that we want the public to perceive AI self-driving cars in a freakish manner.

There might be a fine line then between purposely coming up with a common or standard scheme of shapes or colors that could make an AI self-driving car become readily apparent to humans, and especially pedestrians, and yet also not be overly garish. A kind of softer disruptive camouflage, as it were.

Unlike the normal kind of disruptive camouflage that intends to deceive about speed and direction, we'd of course want the razzle dazzle to make those factors actually more apparent, rather than less so. Also, the traditional disruptive camouflage for navy ships is distinct per ship so that the class of ships cannot be revealed, while in this case we would want something that was consistent across all instances. In that sense, please use this analogy to the disruptive camouflage concept in a thoughtful manner and not a stricter aspect-for-aspect manner.

Presumably, each auto maker would want to be able to still provide their own look-and-feel to the AI self-driving car, allowing them to be differentiated in the marketplace.

A pedestrian might take more notice of an AI self-driving car if it had some kind of standardized markings or indication, and hopefully the pedestrian would be more cautious accordingly. This though also raises the other side of the coin, namely that pedestrians might purposely try to prank an AI self-driving car, and by knowing right away that the car coming down the street is an AI self-driving car, they might more readily be apt to play such tricks.

If we don't do something to make AI self-driving cars appear distinctive, it essentially means that they will be using traditional "camouflage" in that they will blend into the surroundings consisting of other conventional cars.

You won't be able to readily notice whether those cars nearby are human driven or AI self-driving cars. As a society, do we believe that AI self-driving cars should be required to appear distinctive, or are we fine with them blending in? Razzle dazzle, or just the norm. Time will tell.

.

CHAPTER 9
REWILDING
OF
AI SELF-DRIVING CARS

CHAPTER 9

REWILDING

OF

AI SELF-DRIVING CARS

The great outdoors. Every once and a while it's a nice change of pace to get outside of the hustle and bustle of the city and take in some fresh scenery. Within just a few hours' drive of Los Angeles there are some notable forests that are teaming with animals. You can climb rock walls, stand in waterfalls, and enjoy the clean air and the mix with the local wildlife.

If you aren't trained as a botanist or biologist or ecologist, you might not be aware that many of these seemingly unspoiled forested lands are actually quite marred by the hands of mankind. It might not seem so upon first glance. A keen eye though can discern that the biodiversity is at times a fraction of what it was before mankind started to "invade" these pristine areas. For example, in many cases the top predators in that ecosystem are likely expunged or near to being eradicated from the area. A higher level of predator has managed to scoot out these others, namely the arrival of civilized mankind, the ultimate predator (well, except for maybe the one that Arnold Schwarzenegger fought in the now-classic 1987 movie!).

In some areas, there is a concerted effort to reinstate the earlier status quo of those lands. This involves not only protecting what is there, but also includes doing a systematic restoration to the wilderness too. There are specialists that refer to this as wildlife reengineering. A wildlife engineer studies the existing state of the ecosystem and tries to devise a means to re-introduce wildlife into it. The goal is to do this in a fashion that the ecosystem ultimately becomes self-regulating and self-sustaining. Mankind tries to push it toward a true wildlife wilderness and then hopefully steps aside and doesn't need to continually be in the middle of doing so (other than providing further protection from mankind itself).

There's a term that has arisen for this process of re-instituting the wilds to a wilderness state, namely it is called rewilding.

Keep in mind that not everyone believes in the notion of rewilding. Some opponents say that mankind is part of nature and so it is already "natural" that the ecosystem has changed because of mankind's presence. Trying to somehow restore the wild to a pre-mankind arrival doesn't make much sense to them. Even if you could do such a restoration, are you then going to ban humans from going into these restored wild areas? Denying human access seems like a rather nutty option, in their view.

Proponents toward rewilding tend to say that they are not trying to remove mankind from the equation, and only trying to undo the damages that mankind has wrought. They say that we all now know more about what kind of adverse impacts the introduction of mankind can have. This will allow for the revived ecosystem to co-exist with mankind, in which mankind now takes better care as to how the interaction with the wilderness takes place. Few of the proponents say mankind should be banned and instead argue that there should instead be limits and regulations on what mankind can do in the wild, trying to in essence save mankind's base instincts from itself.

You might have seen some of the wildlife overpass crossings that are put up over highways that run through a wilderness area. This is an example, some say, of a rewilding tactic. The wildlife overpass crossing is made to be as natural and nature-like as feasible, including having trees, plants, grass, and so on. Animals that might have otherwise tried to cross the actual highway, and be struck by human's driving their cars, will hopefully tend to use the specially constructed overpass crossing instead.

Notice in this example that the highway was not removed from the wilderness, though of course some rewilders would want that aspect to occur. Instead a kind of "compromise" was found that aids the wildlife and still aids mankind. One could also say that the overpass saves human lives. It presumably is a win-win, allowing for some amount of rewilding and yet also retaining mankind's interest in the wilderness area.

As in any endeavor, there are some proponents of rewilding that are at the extreme end and would say that the use of an overpass is not even considered a form of rewilding. To them, true rewilding would consist of routing that highway to avoid the wilderness entirely. One question that arises by those that are sympathetic to such notions and yet also have some qualms, involves the cost for doing such rewilding. A large-scale full-scale rewilding of an enormous wilderness is not going to be cheap. Where will the money come from to fund such an enterprise?

Proponents of rewilding would say that we all owe the wilderness for the prior transgressions of our ancestors. Like it or not, we need to now share the cost to put the wild back into the wilderness. And though I previously mentioned forests, the "wild" refers to any kind of biome or habitat, whether it is a forest, a desert, and so on. Some consider conservationists to be rewilders, while others suggest that you can be a conservationist and not necessarily be a rewilder -- or at least have varying views on the topic of rewilding.

What does this have to do with AI self-driving cars?

At the Cybernetic AI Self-Driving Car Institute, we are developing AI software for self-driving cars. Our view is that there are several eras underlying the evolution of AI self-driving cars, and one of those eras will involve the "rewilding" of AI self-driving cars.

Allow me to elaborate.

I'd like to clarify and introduce the notion that there are varying levels of AI self-driving cars. The topmost level is considered Level 5. A Level 5 self-driving car is one that is being driven by the AI and

151

there is no human driver involved. For the design of Level 5 self-driving cars, the auto makers are even removing the gas pedal, brake pedal, and steering wheel, since those are contraptions used by human drivers. The Level 5 self-driving car is not being driven by a human and nor is there an expectation that a human driver will be present in the self-driving car. It's all on the shoulders of the AI to drive the car.

For self-driving cars less than a Level 5, there must be a human driver present in the car. The human driver is currently considered the responsible party for the acts of the car. The AI and the human driver are co-sharing the driving task. In spite of this co-sharing, the human is supposed to remain fully immersed into the driving task and be ready at all times to perform the driving task. I've repeatedly warned about the dangers of this co-sharing arrangement and predicted it will produce many untoward results.

Let's focus herein on the true Level 5 self-driving car. Much of the comments apply to the less than Level 5 self-driving cars too, but the fully autonomous AI self-driving car will receive the most attention in this discussion.

Here's the usual steps involved in the AI driving task:

- Sensor data collection and interpretation
- Sensor fusion
- Virtual world model updating
- AI action planning
- Car controls command issuance

Up until current times, most of the work on AI self-driving cars has been primarily research oriented, often done by university research labs and other government related entities. Some would say this was the "pre-historic" era of AI self-driving cars, though I think using such language as "pre-historic" is a disservice to those that have done incredible work to get us to where we are today.

Today's era might be characterized as the Exploratory era.

As a result of a grand convergence of key factors, the advent of AI self-driving cars is beginning to emerge. It isn't going to just suddenly up and appear. Instead, it will be years of trial efforts. I've mentioned many times that there will be hard times ahead for AI self-driving cars during this experimentation and exploratory period.

Will the public be willing to endure the hardships that will occur as AI self-driving cars get involved in untoward incidents on our roadways? Will they tolerate such instances, or will it draw their ire and might there be a backlash that generates onerous regulations that dampen the efforts toward true Level 5 self-driving cars?

I've predicted that we'll make it through the Exploratory Era, and we'll then move into the Taming Era.

During the Taming era, there will be a socio-technical interplay of how the auto makers and tech firms devise and shape the AI of self-driving cars, along with the public and regulators, doing so to arrive at a "tamed" version of Level 5 self-driving cars. Numerous hearings will take place. Advocacy groups that are today rather subdued on the matter will come forth and be quite outspoken. There will be sides taken as to pro-AI self-driving car versus opposed to AI self-driving cars.

By this somewhat acrimonious process, there will be a kind of "taming" of AI self-driving cars. By the word taming I'm referring to the kinds of driving capabilities that the AI self-driving cars will possess.

Right now, most of the auto makers and tech firms are creating rather timid AI drivers. In some sense, you might liken this to a novice teenage driver. When a teenage driver first starts to drive a car, they usually tend to come to a stop at a stop sign and take a seemingly long time to look around before they proceed. They tend to drive at or below the speed limit. You've perhaps found yourself behind one of these novice drivers and gotten frustrated that they are driving with such a sluggish pace and in a rather timid manner.

For AI self-driving cars, given the rudimentary and rather crude capabilities of today's versions, it certainly makes sense that the AI will be driving in a similar timid manner. The public is already on-edge about whether to trust AI self-driving cars. It won't take too many incidents of an AI self-driving car that injures or kills someone, whether it be human occupants in the self-driving car or humans outside of the self-driving car, and the public support for AI self-driving cars will wane quickly.

So, we'll migrate from the Exploratory era to the Taming era, which will achieve finding a balance between having AI self-driving cars on our roadways and have them function in a manner that is more akin to a smoothened novice driver rather than a more seasoned sophisticated driver.

Some believe for example that an AI self-driving car should always drive in a purely legal manner. This idea that AI self-driving cars would need to strictly adhere to the legal requirements for driving a car will inhibit the kind of driving that we already accept by humans. In essence, if the AI is going to only be able to drive in a strictly legal fashion, you are by definition going to limit the savviness of the driving by the AI.

I'd anticipate that we'll have reached a point that the public generally accepts the use of AI self-driving cars on our roadways. People will find these tamed AI self-driving cars to be reasonably acceptable for use among the general public. It will be as though we've all agreed to let teenagers drive cars and even though we'll realize they aren't going to improve much over time, at least they are consistent in the tamed nature of how they are driving. Being a predictable driver is handy, even if the driver is timid and tentative as to how they drive.

When I mention that the AI self-driving car won't improve much over time, I am not saying that this is due to the limits of the AI per se. Instead, I am suggesting that since the tamed or timid nature of the AI has been arrived at as a societal preference, the boundaries will be established not so much by what the AI can actually do, but more so by what society is willing to allow for the AI to do.

Don't though over-state that aspect, since I am not saying that the AI will be able to drive miraculously, and it is somehow artificially being held back. There will be a crossover point of the further maturation of the AI and the limits imposed by society as part of the taming period.

Keep in mind too that there will be a mix of both human driven cars and AI self-driving cars during this period of time. I realize that there are pundits that say we will only have AI self-driving cars, but this belies the aspect that today we have about 200+ million cars in the United States, and there is nothing that will somehow overnight change those into AI self-driving cars.

For many years, there will be a mix of human driven cars and AI self-driving cars. I point this out because the utopians envision a world in which cars are all communicating and coordinating with each other, and there is zero chance of fatalities due to automobile incidents. It really doesn't make much sense to be discussing this all-and-only AI self-driving cars world since it is a far distant future, and instead be more practical and face the reality of a world composed of both human driven cars and AI self-driving cars.

What kind of driving won't the tamed AI do?

Imagine you are on the freeway. If you are a human driver, and you are heading to work for the day, you might be willing to weave in-and-out of the traffic, trying to make headway in an otherwise somewhat crowded freeway. The AI of the self-driving cars for the Tamed Era will instead tend to stay in their lane, and only make a lane change when actually required. Thus, the AI made a lane change to get say onto the freeway, and maybe made another lane change to the fast lane since the distance to work is far enough to warrant getting into the fast lane. Once the exit nears, the AI instructs the self-driving car to move over lanes to make the exit.

In that sense, the AI is being "held back" from driving in a manner that a human would drive. Presumably, if the AI is as good as a human driver, it should be able to weave in-and-out of the traffic, just as a human would. I realize there are risks associated with this kind of driving tactic, and I'm not suggesting that the weaving approach is necessarily good, but on the other hand it does have some advantages and provides a driving technique that when used sensibly can be helpful.

With today's AI, it would be prudent to not trust a self-driving car to do this kind of weaving tactic. The AI is just not good enough as yet. It would be similar to telling a teenage novice driver to weave throughout traffic on the freeway. I think we would all shudder at the prospects of such an act. The odds are that the weaving would as a minimum disturb the rest of the traffic, and more than likely lead to a car incident of one kind or another.

Eventually, the AI is going to be good enough to do this kind of weaving. But, we as a society will not be ready for it and will instead need to undergo the Taming Era to have sufficient belief and faith that AI self-driving cars can at least handle the rudiments of driving on our roadways.

It is at this juncture that the third era will arise, the Rewilding Era.

I've opted to call this third era the "rewilding" period because in some sense we are going to be returning AI self-driving cars back to what was originally envisioned. It was envisioned that AI self-driving cars would drive as proficiently as humans. This includes the various day-to-day tricks that we humans use. It includes the borderline legal maneuvers that humans use when driving. It involves perhaps some degree of illegal driving that humans use today. And so on.

We'll shift from the tamed AI self-driving car to the rewilded AI self-driving car. I'm not going to say that the AI self-driving cars will be "wild" per se, and indeed I don't think we would want them to be driving in a crazy or foolish or senseless way. Instead, I'm suggesting that we'll take off the earlier imposed limits and allow the AI to flourish and drive the self-driving car in a manner more consistent with the "wild" way in which humans drive a car.

In a manner of speaking, you might say that we'll be putting a tiger in the tank of AI self-driving cars.

For those of you that don't recall, one of history's most well-known advertising campaigns occurred during the 1960's and involved a slogan that you should put a tiger in your tank. It became a quite popular saying and did well for the Esso gasoline provider. Eventually, the phrase itself became commonplace as an expression of getting energized.

Here then are the three eras of AI self-driving cars:

1) Exploratory Era (today)

2) Taming Era (coming up)

3) Rewilding Era (post-Taming)

We will progress from today's Exploratory Era into the Taming Era. This will allow us as a society to generally become accepting of AI self-driving cars. Once that has occurred, there will be an impetus to shift toward the third era, the Rewilding Era. At that juncture, the AI will be sophisticated enough that it will be time to take-off the training wheels, so to speak, and let it roll.

I'd say it is premature right now to be telling people that someday we'll be putting a tiger in their tank and making AI self-driving cars become aggressive human-like drivers. Unless you've first lived in the Taming Era, there is little chance you can readily perceive that there's a further future ahead for AI self-driving cars that involves such driving tactics. We'll need to ease our way into it. That's fine, though, and provides breathing room for the AI to get better suited for driving, and become in some sense just like those maniac human "driving tigers" that we all are.

CHAPTER 10
BRUTE FORCE ALGORITHMS
AND
AI SELF-DRIVING CARS

Lance B. Eliot

160

CHAPTER 10

BRUTE FORCE ALGORITHMS
AND
AI SELF-DRIVING CARS

When my children were young, they used to enjoy playing hide-and-seek with each other. One of them would hide somewhere either in the house or in our yard and be allowed a few minutes to find a good hiding spot. Once the other one had finished waiting the prescribed time period, the search would begin. At times, the search was quite hilarious to watch, particularly when they were quite young, since the places looked into were not at all feasible for any of them to hide in. I recall at one point that the teapot was examined and, on another occasion, that a potted plant in the house was dug into as though perhaps the hider might have become a gopher and dug into the dirt.

The search also at first covered every square inch of the house and the yard. They each would usually start indoors and go from room to room, looking throughout the bedroom of the other, then the bathroom, then their own bedroom, then the living room, then the kitchen, etc. If the hider wasn't found in the house, the search would continue outdoors. This outdoor search usually began in the backyard, then went to the side yard, and eventually to the front yard.

There were some rules about the game that made things "fairer" in that the hider could not change their hiding spot during the game, and nor could they hide in a location that was considered out-of-bounds (for example, we banned them from climbing on the roof, that kind of thing). The person searching had to dutifully conduct the search. I mention this aspect because one tactic they discovered was the searcher could just sit and watch TV and figured that the hider would get tired of waiting to be found and voluntarily give themselves up. That wasn't the spirit of the game.

All in all, they typically would conduct a rather exhaustive search.

It used up a chunk of their play time and perhaps honed their cognitive ability to undertake a reasoned approach to solving a problem. I enjoyed seeing that they were able to during a search proceed without backtracking and usually avoided revisiting the same location twice. If they felt that they had done an exhaustive search in a particular location, let's say in the kitchen, they reasoned that there was no need to come back to the kitchen to do so again (recall that the hider could not be sneaky and move from location to location, which of course if so would then potentially necessitate revisiting prior search locations).

They also discovered that if they were sloppy about doing the search, they might end-up having apparently looked everywhere and yet still not found the hider. This was met with great chagrin as it implied that the searcher had somehow overlooked the hiding spot of the hider. At times, if one of them had looked inside and outside and could not find the hider, they would make an accusation that the hider had violated the rules and gone out-of-bounds. An out-of-bounds player was automatically considered the "loser" of the game and forfeited the game to the searcher. As parents, we also added additional penalties to going out-of-bounds since we didn't want the children to unknowingly in their innocent desperation hide in a spot that would be dangerous for them (e.g., hiding in the fireplace was not allowed, likewise no hiding behind the furnace).

As they grew a bit older, and after having played the game many times, they improved upon their search techniques. One of the overarching aspects of the search involved whether to begin by searching inside the house versus outside of the house. They had each fallen into a pattern of always starting inside the house. This used up a lot of time as they went from room to room. The hider often realized that they could last longer in terms of hiding by finding a spot outside, and it was considered better to be hidden longer rather than getting caught right away. Also, living in Southern California, the outside weather was usually nice and sunny, so hiding outdoors was generally more enjoyable anyway.

As a result of these aspects, the searcher would often decide to forego starting the search indoors and instead begin it outdoors. This seemed like a prudent improvement to the search effort. Why not start the search where you believe the chances of finding the hider are heightened?

This handy rule-of-thumb had its uses and yet was not considered an iron clad approach. If the weather was somewhat foul, the odds were that the hider would opt to hide inside. In that case, rather than shifting to search outdoors first, it made more sense to instead search indoors first.

Likewise, they began to realize that the places of hiding had to be large enough to accommodate the hider. Sure, the hider could scrunch themselves up if needed, or maybe even try to stretch themselves out, but in any case, it was realized that they could not somehow fit into a teapot. There were plentiful areas both indoors and outdoors that could accommodate a hider, and meanwhile there were many more areas that obviously could not accommodate a hider.

Another rule of the game was that the hider could not disturb anything in order to hide. For example, you could not pull things out of a closet to make space for you to hide in closet. If the closet had space within which you could fit, it was permissible to hide in there, but you could not be moving things around to create a space where none already existed per se.

Eventually, the game lost its attraction. There were only so many places to hide and it became apparent as to where those spots were. The job of the searcher became focused solely on going to those spots. There was no need to run all around the house and no need to run all around the yard. Just quickly go to each of the known hiding spots, and you could rather expeditiously find the hider. Furthermore, you could usually guess which of those spots the hider might actually use, since there were some spots more accommodating and desirable than others (hiding behind the stinky cat liter box was not on the top of the list of places to hide!).

As an AI developer, I was fascinated in the evolution of their playing this hide-and-seek game. When they were young and first discovering how to play the game, they pretty much did an exhaustive kind of search. Look everywhere. Leave no stone unturned. Just start looking and keep looking until you find the hider. It involved a lot of exciting and playful running around the house and the yard.

Brute force.

That's a phrase that would aptly describe their initial approach to playing the hide-and-seek game. The notion of brute force is that you undertake an exhaustive effort towards trying to do something. In the case of the kids, they would begin looking and just keep looking until they found the hider. All rooms were included, and all of the outdoor yard area was included.

As mentioned, at first, they had no particular strategy to how they were doing the search. It was almost a mindless kind of approach. Explore all possibilities was the mantra. When you find the hider, you are done.

The nice thing about a brute force method or algorithm is that it is usually pretty easy to implement and describe. I'm going to start looking for the hider and continue doing so until they are found and will look high and low to find them. This search process of looking high and low included areas that would not even accommodate the hider.

One of the disadvantages of a brute force approach is that it can be inefficient. The children would run throughout all rooms of the house and yet there were some rooms that had no available hiding spots. They at first always looked inside the house, even though the odds were that the hider was likely hiding outside. They looked in spots that would not even accommodate the hider. All of this was a quite inefficient search process (but, they had a lot of fun!).

Imagine if you had a computer that was undertaking some kind of search among a lot of data. You could use a brute force method to do so. Similar to the children and their hide-and-seek game, the computer could just start looking and continue doing so until it finds whatever is being searched for. No effort might be undertaken to help the computer identify where to first start looking and nor whether it can skip some of the data that might be readily inapplicable to the matter. Instead, the brute force might look at each data element, one by one, one after another, doing so exhaustively.

From a programming perspective, the odds are that the programmer that opts to use a brute force approach doesn't have to do much work in terms of preparing the code for the effort. It tends to be easy to write such code. When I say easy, I mean that in comparison to having come up with a more elaborated method takes more effort to do. If you want to have a computer routine that will be savvy in doing a search, it takes some thinking about what the method should be. You need to design it and then code it. You need to test it to figure out whether it works or not. And so on.

One potential issue with brute force is that it can be difficult to know whether the brutish method will be able to find the desired solution in a "reasonable" amount of time.

Suppose the kids had a timeclock that kept track of their hide-and-seek game. If they had agreed to limit the search time to say five minutes, and if the approach of going throughout the entire house was taking say six minutes, it would imply that they would have only had time to do the indoors search and not the outdoors search. Furthermore, the six minutes to do the indoors search would have to end at the five minute deadline, meaning that even the indoor search would not necessarily complete.

For a computer system, using a brute force algorithm, it might take minutes, hours, days, weeks, months, or might not ever end (assuming you could let it keep running), while trying to find the solution being sought. This could chew-up a lot of processing cycles too. You could potentially devote a computer entirely to this search task and it might consume all available computing cycles in doing so.

Often times, when considering computer systems, you need to look at both the processing cycles consumed and the amount of computer memory consumed too. A brute force method can make use of computer processing cycles during its efforts. This might also require the use of computer memory while doing so.

Memory can be consumed at a tremendous rate during a brute force method. One danger then of a brute force approach is that it can consume so much memory that it might use up all available memory for the computer system being used. This could cause the brute force method to falter, and in some cases come to a halt prematurely.

Oddly enough, a brute force method can actually be a low memory consumer. In other words, rather than using up a lot of memory, the brute force algorithm might use hardly any memory at all. The simplistic nature of the algorithm might be that it uses a minimal amount of memory to undertake its steps. In contrast, sometimes a savvy algorithm might use up a lot of memory, doing so as a means of reducing the time required to find a solution.

If the time performance of a brute force computer algorithm is maybe taking too long, there are ways to potentially speed up the brute force effort without having to change the algorithm itself. For example, you might be able to use a faster computer processor. You might be able to add more computer memory. You might see if you can parallelize it, doing so by perhaps deploying the algorithm onto multiple processors.

The parallelization is not so easy a means to speed-up things. The nature of the brute force algorithm might not lend itself to working in parallel. As such, you cannot blindly just toss more processors at the situation and hope that it will help. The added processors might not speed up things and might actually be unused since there's no clear-cut way to parallelize without changing the algorithm.

There's a fine line between pure brute force and trying to make the brute force a bit savvier. Remember when the children realized that they might be better off to start their search outside, since they knew that it was an often-used hiding spot. Maybe we can improve a pure brute force method by refining it.

Some refer to this as employing brute reason.

It can be hard to say where the dividing line is between a pure brute force versus adding brute reasoning, and also then extending beyond brute reasoning to say that we are using a non-brute force method entirely.

With the kids, they might have been using "brute reasoning" when they opted to search outdoors at first rather than indoors and they no longer looked in spots that could not accommodate a hider. You might say they progressed beyond brute reasoning and into a non-brute force method when they began to use their awareness of where the hider was more likely to hide, and not look in every room and reduce the overall search space size accordingly.

Indeed, we tend to think of brute force as a means to search a search space. If the search space is very large, the brute force method, though perhaps easy to implement, might then be quite lengthy in trying to find the desired solution. The kids added various rules-of-thumb, which we might call heuristics, and for which it then "reduced" the amount of search space that had to be examined (no longer looking at all rooms and all possible hiding spots).

What does this have to do with AI self-driving cars?

At the Cybernetic AI Self-Driving Cars Institute, we are developing AI software for self-driving cars. One crucial aspect of the AI involves its ability to perform various searches.

You might be thinking of searches when driving a car such as trying to figure out how to get to where you are going. Maybe there are ten different ways that you can drive to work. Which of the ten paths would be the best? You might use a computer algorithm to consider each of the ten paths. Some might of the paths might be shorter than others, but those shorter paths might involve lots of intersections with traffic signals, all of which might increase the driving time even if the distance is not as far.

There are other various kinds of searches that take place.

Allow me to elaborate.

I'd like to first clarify and introduce the notion that there are varying levels of AI self-driving cars. The topmost level is considered Level 5. A Level 5 self-driving car is one that is being driven by the AI and there is no human driver involved. For the design of Level 5 self-driving cars, the auto makers are even removing the gas pedal, brake pedal, and steering wheel, since those are contraptions used by human drivers. The Level 5 self-driving car is not being driven by a human and nor is there an expectation that a human driver will be present in the self-driving car. It's all on the shoulders of the AI to drive the car.

For self-driving cars less than a Level 5, there must be a human driver present in the car. The human driver is currently considered the responsible party for the acts of the car. The AI and the human driver are co-sharing the driving task. In spite of this co-sharing, the human is supposed to remain fully immersed into the driving task and be ready at all times to perform the driving task. I've repeatedly warned about the dangers of this co-sharing arrangement and predicted it will produce many untoward results.

Let's focus herein on the true Level 5 self-driving car. Much of the comments apply to the less than Level 5 self-driving cars too, but the fully autonomous AI self-driving car will receive the most attention in this discussion.

Here's the usual steps involved in the AI driving task:

- Sensor data collection and interpretation
- Sensor fusion
- Virtual world model updating
- AI action planning
- Car controls command issuance

During the driving task, the AI system is collecting data from the myriad of sensors, including radar, sonic, cameras, LIDAR, and others. The data needs to be explored to try and identify what the data indicates.

For example, suppose that the camera has captured a picture of the scene in front of the self-driving car. The AI needs to examine the picture and try to see if there are other cars up ahead. Are there pedestrians nearby the self-driving car? Are there bicyclists nearby the self-driving car? All of these have to be found in the picture. Likewise, for the radar, sonic results, LIDAR data, a search needs to be made to figure out what objects exist in that data.

Brute force.

Brute force would be one way to conduct the search of the sensory collected data. The computer on-board the self-driving car could exhaustively examine the data. This might seem like a sensible approach. Just have the system look at everything and anything.

But, suppose the amount of time it takes to do this brute force examination of the sensory data took three seconds to undertake. Suppose the self-driving car was moving along at 55 miles per hour, which is about 80 feet per second. In the three seconds that the brute force algorithm was looking at the data, the self-driving car has moved 240 feet. In that distance, it could be that the self-driving car rams into another car ahead, doing so because the AI was not yet aware that a car was directly ahead and that the AI ought to hit the brakes on the self-driving car.

As such, using a simplistic brute force algorithm might be "easy" to implement, but it could also have life-or-death consequences. Driving a car is a real-time task that requires being extremely mindful of the clock.

You might be tempted to suggest that perhaps we can speed-up the data exploration by adding more processors to the on-board computer systems. It might help, it might not. As mentioned before, parallelization is not an automatic due to just adding more processors.

Plus, you need to consider the added cost to the self-driving car, which would be boosted by adding more processors, or faster processors, or adding more memory.

Not only would adding more hardware increase the costs associated with the self-driving car, it would add weight and take up more space in the self-driving car. By adding weight to a self-driving car, you are potentially impacting its overall size and maneuverability. The use of space in the self-driving car would likely reduce available space for other purposes, such as space for the human occupants that would likely be wanting to ride in the self-driving car.

There are other important and time critical aspects of the driving task for the AI.

The AI system is keeping track of a virtual world model. This is a kind of 3D virtual representation of the surroundings of the self-driving car. The AI needs to use this virtual model to try and anticipate what it should do next, and what else might occur next in the surrounding environment. Is that car to your right going to try and get ahead of the self-driving car and barge into the lane of the self-driving car? Is that bicyclist that's riding in the bike lane going to potentially swerve out of the bike lane and into the path of the self-driving car?

You might think of the analysis of the virtual world model as a game of chess. In chess, you need to consider what your next move consists of. Furthermore, you need to consider what counter-moves might take place after your next move. You can do this for a series of levels of thinking ahead, called ply. How many ply ahead should you look when playing chess? Usually, the more ply, the better your current move will be chosen.

While the AI is driving the self-driving car, it needs to carefully explore the virtual world model. The AI might tentatively decide that a right turn would be prudent at the next corner. But, suppose further examination of the virtual world model reveals that the right corner is blocked with red cones and there is construction work taking place there. This might preclude taking a right turn at the corner. The AI would then need to reassess and figure out what might be the next best move, perhaps waiting to make a right turn later on or perhaps making a series of left turns to get to where it needs to go.

Brute force.

Would it make sense to explore the virtual model on a pure brute force approach? The issue is similar to the points made earlier, namely whether a brute force algorithm could work quickly enough and thoroughly enough to get the job done in time. Likely not.

As a result, it is crucial that these kinds of AI systems be using at least brute reasoning, and more so that they would be using very savvy heuristics. A wide variety of AI techniques are utilized, such as using machine learning, support vector machines, etc.

At some of my presentations about AI self-driving cars, I at times have programmers that seem to wonder why the AI software for a self-driving car is so complex. For some of these programmers, they think that the programming should be straightforward. I point out that if we could just use simplistic brute force methods, it would reduce the complexity of the software and make getting the software established much easier and faster. Unfortunately, due to the nature of the driving task, a brute force approach is unlikely to be insufficient. It would not work adequately under the severe time constraints involved in driving a car. For the programmer's toolkit, having brute force algorithms at the ready is handy, but they should only be used when appropriate. The AI systems for self-driving cars require much more than brute force.

Lance B. Eliot

172

CHAPTER 11

IDLE MOMENTS

AND

AI SELF-DRIVING CARS

CHAPTER 11

IDLE MOMENTS

AND

AI SELF-DRIVING CARS

Have you ever been sitting at a red light and your mind goes into idle, perhaps daydreaming about that vacation to Hawaii that you'd like to take, but meanwhile you are there in your car and heading to work once again. I'm sure all of us have "zoned out" from time-to-time while driving our cars. It's obviously not an advisable thing to do. In theory, your mind should always be on alert while you are sitting in the driver's seat.

Some of my colleagues that drive for hours each day due to their jobs are apt to say that you cannot really be on full-alert for every moment of your driving. They insist that a bit of a mental escape from the driving task is perfectly fine, assuming that you do so when the car is otherwise not doing something active. Sitting at a red light is usually a rather idle task for the car and the car driver. You need to keep your foot on the brake pedal and be ready to switch over to the gas pedal once the light goes green. Seems like that's about it.

In such a case, as long as you are steadfast in keeping your foot on the brake pedal while at the red light, presumably your mind can wander to other matters. You might be thinking about what you are going to have for dinner that night. You might be calculating how much you owe on your mortgage and trying to ascertain when you'll have it entirely paid off. You might be thinking about that movie you saw last week and how the plot and the actors were really good. In essence, your mind might be on just about anything – and it is likely anything other than the car and driving of the car at that moment in time.

Some of you might claim that even if your mind has drifted from the driving task, it's never really that far away. You earnestly believe that in a split second you could be mentally utterly engaged in the driving task, if there was a need to do so. My colleagues say that they believe that when driving and in-motion they are devoting maybe 90% of the minds to the driving task (the other 10% is used for daydreaming or other non-car driving mental pondering). Meanwhile, when at a red light, they are using maybe 10% of their mind to the driving task and the rest can be used for more idle thoughts. To them, the 10% is sufficient. They are sure that they can ramp-up from the sitting still 10% to the 90% active-driver mentally and do so to handle whatever might arise.

We can likely all agree that while at a red light there is still a chance of something going amiss. Yes, most of the time you just sit still, and your car is not moving. The other cars directly around you might also be in a similar posture. You might have cars to your left, and to your right, and ahead of you, and behind you, all of whom are sitting still and also waiting for the red light to turn green. You are so boxed in that even if you wanted to take some kind action with your car, you don't have much room to move. You are landlocked.

Those that do not allow their thoughts to go toward more idle mental chitchat are perhaps either obsessive drivers or maybe don't have much else they want to be thinking about. There is the category of drivers that find themselves mentally taxed by the driving task overall. For example, teenage novice drivers are often completely consumed by the arduous nature of the driving task. Even if they wanted to think about their baseball practice or that homework that's due tonight, they are often so new to the driver's seat and so worried about getting into an accident that they put every inch of their being towards driving the car. Especially when it's their parent's car.

By-and-large, I'd be willing to bet that most of the seasoned drivers out there are prone to mental doodling whenever the car comes to a situation permitting it. Sitting at a red light is one of the most obvious examples. Another would be waiting in a long line of cars, such as trying to get into a crowded parking lot and all of the cars are stopped momentarily, waiting for some other driver to park their car and thus allow traffic to flow again. We have lots of car driving moments wherein the car is at a standstill and there's not much to do but wait for the car ahead of you to get moving.

Many drivers also stretch the idling car mental freedom moments and include circumstances whereby the car is crawling forward, albeit at a low speed. Presumably, you should not be thinking about anything other than the driving task, and though maybe there might be a carve out for when the car is completely motionless, it's another aspect altogether to be doing idle thinking when the car is actually in motion. I was inching my way up an on-ramp onto the freeway this morning, and all of the cars were going turtle speeds while dealing with the excessive number of cars that all were trying to use the same on-ramp. We definitely were not motionless. It was a very slow crawl.

I noticed that the car ahead of me seemed to not be flowing at the same inching along speed as the rest of us. The car would come almost to a complete halt, and then with the few inches now between it and the car ahead, it would jerk forward to cover the ground. It happened repeatedly. This was a not very smooth way to inch along. My guess was that the driver was distracted by something else, maybe listening to a radio station or computing Fibonacci numbers mentally, and so was doing a staggered approach to the on-ramp traffic situation.

At least twice, the driver nearly bumped into the car that was ahead of it. This happened because the driver was doing this seemingly idiotic stop-and-go approach, rather than doing what the rest of us were doing, namely an even and gradual crawling forward motion. The car ahead of that driver seemed to realize too that they were almost getting bumped from behind. Several times, the car ahead put on their brake lights, as though trying to warn the other driver to watch out and not hit them. In theory, nobody had to be touching their brakes, since we all could have been crawling at the same speed and kept our respective distances from each other.

I hope you would agree that if indeed the driver was mentally distracted, they were doing so in a dicey situation. Once cars are in-motion, the odds of something going astray tend to increase. In fact, you might even say that the odds increase exponentially. The car that's motionless, assuming it's in a situation that normally has motionless involved, likely can allow more latitude for that mentally distracted driver.

Notice that I mentioned the motionless car in the context of motionlessness being expected. If you are driving down a busy street and suddenly jam on the brakes and come to a halt, in spite of your now being motionless, it would seem that your danger factor is going to be quite high. Sure, your car is motionless, but it happened in a time and place that was unexpected to other drivers. As such, those other drivers are bound to ram into your car. Imagine someone that just mentally discovered the secret to those finger licking good herbs and spices, and they were so taken by their own thoughts that they arbitrarily hit the brakes of their car and out-of-the-blue came to a stop on the freeway. Not a good idea.

So far, we've covered the aspect that when your car is motionless in an expected situation of motionless that you are apt to let your mind wander and turn towards idle thoughts, doing so while the car itself is presumably idling. We'll acknowledge that something untoward can still happen, and there's a need to remain involved in the driving task. Some people maybe reduce their mental driving consumption a bit lower than we might all want, and there's a danger that the person is not at all ready for a sudden and unexpected disruption to the motionless.

What does all of this have to do with AI self-driving cars?

At the Cybernetic AI Self-Driving Car Institute, we are developing AI systems for self-driving cars. As part of that effort, we also are considering how to best utilize the AI and the processors on-board a self-driving car during so-called idle moments.

Allow me to elaborate.

Your AI self-driving car comes up to a red light. It stops. It is boxed in by other surrounding cars that have also come to a normal stop at the red light. This is similar to a human driver car and the situation that I was using earlier as an example of idle moments. Nothing unusual about this. You might not even realize that the car next to you is an AI self-driving car. It is just patiently motionless, like the other nearby cars, and presumably waiting for that green light to appear.

Here's a good question for you — what should the AI being doing at that moment in time?

I think we can all agree that at least the AI should be observing what's going on around the self-driving car and be anticipating the green light. Sure, that would be standard operating procedure (SOP). A human would (should) be doing the same. Got it.

Suppose though that this effort to be looking around and anticipating the green light was able to be done without using up fully the available set of computational resources available to the AI system that's on-board the self-driving car. You might liken this to a human driver that believes they are only using a fraction of their mental capacity for driving purposes when sitting at a red light. The human assumes that they can use some remainder of their underutilized mental prowess during these idle moments.

For many of the auto makers and tech firms, they right now are not seeking to leverage these idle moments for other purposes. To them, this is considered an "edge" problem. An edge problem in computer science is one that is considered at the periphery or edge of what you are otherwise trying to solve. The auto makers and tech firms are focused on the core right now of having an AI self-driving car that can drive a car down a road, stop at a red light, and proceed when the light is green.

If there are untapped or "wasted" computational cycles that could have been used during an "idle" moment, so be it. No harm, no foul, with respect to the core aspects of the driving task. Might it be "nice" to leverage those computational resources when they are available?

Sure, but it isn't considered a necessity. Some would argue that you don't need to be going full-blast computationally all of the time and why push things anyway.

When I've brought up this notion of potentially unused capacity, I've had some AI developers make a loud sigh and say that they already have enough on their plates about getting an AI self-driving car to properly drive a car. Forget about doing anything during idle moments other than what's absolutely needed to be done.

They even often will try tossing up some reasons why not to try and use this available time. The easiest retort is that it might distract the AI from the core task of driving the car. To this, we say that it's pretty stupid of anyone considering using the computational excess resources if they are also going to put the core driving task at a disadvantage.

Allow me therefore to immediately and loudly point out that yes, of course, the use of any excess capacity during idle moments is to be done only at the subservient measure to the core driving task. Whatever else the AI is going to do, it must be something that can immediately be stopped or interrupted. Furthermore, it cannot be anything that somehow slows down or stops or interrupts the core aspects of the driving task.

This is what we would expect of a human driver, certainly. A human driver that uses idle moments to think about their desired Hawaiian vacation, would be wrong in doing so if it also meant they were ill-prepared to handle the driving task. I realize that many humans that think they can handle multi-tasking are actually unable to do so, and thus we are all in danger whenever we get on the road. Those drivers that become distracted by other thoughts that are non-driving ones are putting us all at a higher risk of a driving incident. I'd assert that my example of the driver ahead of me on the on-ramp was one such example.

In short, the use of any of the excess available computational resources of an AI self-driving car, during an idle moment, must be only undertaken when it is clear cut that there is such available excess and that it also must not in any manner usurp the core driving task that the AI is expected to undertake.

This can admittedly be trickier than it might seem.

How does the system "know" that the AI effort -- while during an idle moment -- does not need the "excess" computational resources? This is something that per my overall AI self-driving car framework is an important part of the "self-awareness" of the AI system for a self-driving car. This self-awareness capability is right now not being given much due by the auto makers and tech firms developing AI systems for self-driving cars, and as such, it correspondingly provides a reason that trying to use the "excess" is not an easy aspect for their self-driving cars (due to lacking an AI self-awareness to even know when such excess might exist).

The AI of a self-driving car is a real-time system that must continually be aware of time. If the self-driving car is going 75 miles per hour and there's a car up ahead that seems to have lost a tire, how much time does the AI have to figure out what to do? Perhaps there's a component of the AI that can figure out what action to take in this time-critical situation, but suppose the time required for the AI to workout a solution will take longer than is the time available to avoid hitting that car up ahead? There needs to be a self-awareness component of the AI system that is helping to keep track of the time it takes to do things and the time available to get things done.

I'm also focusing my remarks herein toward what are considered true AI self-driving cars, which are ones at a Level 5. A self-driving car of a Level 5 is considered one that the AI is able to drive without any human driver intervention needed and nor expected. The AI must be able to drive the car entirely without human assistance. Indeed, most of the Level 5 self-driving cars are omitting a brake pedal and gas pedal and steering wheel, since those contraptions are for a human driver.

Self-driving cars at a less than Level 5 are considered to co-share the driving task between the human and the AI. In essence, there must be a human driver on-board the self-driving car for a less than Level 5. I've commented many times that this notion of co-sharing the driving task is raft with issues, many of which can lead to confusion and the self-driving car getting into untoward situations. It's not going to be pretty when we have increasingly foul car incidents and in spite of the belief that you can just say the human driver was responsible, I think this will wear thin.

Go along with my indication that there will be a type of firewall between the use of computational resources for the core driving task and those computational resources that might be "excess" and available, and that at any time and without hesitation the core driving task can grab those excess resources.

Some of you that are real-time developers will say that there's overhead for the AI to try and grab the excess resources and thus it would introduce some kind of delay, even if only minuscule. But that any delay, even if minuscule, could make the difference between the core making a life-or-death driving decision.

The counter-argument is that if those excess resources were otherwise sitting entirely idle, it would nonetheless also require overhead to activate those resources. As such, a well-optimized system should not particularly introduce any added delay between the effort to provide unused resources to the core versus resources that were momentarily and temporarily being used. That's a key design aspect.

The next objection from some AI developers is that they offer a cynical remark about how the excess resources might be used. Are you going to use it to calculate pi to the nth degree? Are you going to use it to calculate whether aliens from Mars are beaming messages to us?

This attempt to ridicule the utilization of the excess resources is a bit hollow.

In theory, sure, it could be used to calculate pi and it could be used to detect Martians, since presumably it has no adverse impact on the core driving task. It is similar to the human that's thinking about their Hawaiian vacation, which is presumably acceptable to do as long as it doesn't undermine their driving (which, again, I do agree can undermine their driving, and so the same kind of potential danger could hamper the AI system but we're saying that by design of the AI system that this is being avoided, while with humans it is something essentially unavoidable unless you can redesign the human mind).

How then might we productively use the excess resources when the AI and the core driving task is otherwise at an idle juncture?

One aspect would be to do a double-check of the core driving task. Let's say that the AI is doing a usual sweep of the surroundings, doing so while sitting amongst a bunch of cars that are bunched up at a red light. It's doing this, over and over, wanting to detect anything out of the ordinary. It could be that with the core task there has already been a pre-determined depth of analysis for the AI.

It's like playing a game of chess and trying to decide how many ply or levels to think ahead. You might normally be fine with thinking at four ply and don't have the time or inclination to go much deeper. During the idle moment at a red light, the excess resources might do a kind of double-check and be willing to go to say six ply deep.

The core driving task wasn't expecting the deeper analysis, and nor did it need it per se. On the other hand, a little bit of extra icing on the cake is likely to be potentially helpful. Perhaps the pedestrians that are standing at the corner appear to be standing still and pose no particular "threat" to the AI self-driving car. A deeper analysis might reveal that two of the pedestrians appear poised to move into the street and might do so once the green light occurs. This added analysis could be helpful to the core driving task.

If the excess computational cycles are used for such a purpose and if they don't end-up with enough time to find anything notable, it's nothing lost when you presumably dump it out and continue to use those resources for the core driving task. On the other hand, if perchance there was something found in time, it could be added to the core task awareness and be of potential value.

Another potential use of the excess resource might be to do further planning of the self-driving car journey that is underway.

Perhaps the self-driving car has done an overall path planning for how to get to the destination designated by a human occupant. Suppose the human had said to the self-driving car, get me to Carnegie Hall. At the start of the journey, the AI might have done some preliminary analysis to figure out how to get to the location. This also might be updated during the journey such as if traffic conditions are changing and the AI system becomes informed thereof.

During an otherwise idle moment, there could be more computational effort put towards examining the journey path. This might also involve personalization. Suppose that the human occupant goes this way quite frequently. Perhaps the human has from time-to-time asked the AI to vary the path, maybe due to wanting to stop at a Starbuck s on the way, or maybe due to wanting to see a particular art statute that's on a particular corner along the way. The excess resources might be used to ascertain whether the journey might be taken along a different path.

This also brings up another aspect about the idle moments. If you were in a cab or similar and came to a red light, invariably the human driver is likely to engage you in conversation. How about that football team of ours? Can you believe it's raining again? This is the usual kind of idle conversation. Presumably, the AI could undertake a similar kind of idle conversation with the human occupants of the self-driving car.

Doing this kind of conversation could be fruitful in that it might reveal something else too that the AI self-driving car can assist with. If the human occupant were to say that they are hungering for some coffee, the AI could suggest that the route go in the path that includes a Starbucks. Or, the human occupant might say that they will be returning home that night at 6:00 p.m., and for which the AI might ask then whether the human occupant wants the AI self-driving car to come and pick them up around that time.

There are some that wonder whether the excess resources might be used for other "internal" purposes that might benefit the AI overall of the self-driving car. This could include doing memory-based garbage collection, possibly freeing up space that would otherwise be unavailable during the driving journey (this kind of memory clean-up typically happens after a journey is completed, rather than during a journey). This is a possibility, but it also begins to increase the difficulty of being able to stop it or interrupt it as needed, when so needed.

Likewise, another thought expressed has been to do the OTA (Over The Air) updates during these idle moments. The OTA is used to allow the AI self-driving car to transmit data up to a cloud capability established by the auto maker or tech firm, along with the cloud being able to push down into the AI self-driving car updates and such. The OTA is usually done when the self-driving car is fully motionless, parked, and otherwise not involved in the driving task.

We have to keep in mind that the AI self-driving car during the idle moments being considered herein is still actively on the roadway. It is driving the car. Given today's OTA capabilities, it is likely ill-advised to try and carry out the OTA during such idle moments. This might well change though in the future, depending upon improvements in electronic communications such as 5G, and the advent of edge computing.

Another possibility of the use of the excess resources might be to do some additional Machine Learning during those idle moments. Machine Learning is an essential element of AI self-driving cars and involves the AI system itself being improved over time via a "learning" type of process. For many of the existing AI self-driving cars, the Machine Learning is often relegated to efforts in the cloud by the auto maker or tech firm, and then downloaded into the AI of the self-driving car. This then avoids utilizing the scarce resources of the on-board systems and can leverage the much vaster resources that presumably can be had in the cloud.

If the excess resources during idle moments were used for Machine Learning, it once again increases the dicey nature of using those moments. Can you cut-off the Machine Learning if needed? What aspects of Machine Learning would best be considered for the use of the excess resources. This and a slew of other questions arise. It's not that it isn't feasible, it's just that you'd need to be more mindful about whether this makes sense to have undertaken.

As a few final comments on this topic for now, it is assumed herein that there are excess computational resources during idle moments. This is not necessarily always the case, and indeed on a particular journey it might never be the case. It is quite possible that the AI core driving task will consume all of the resources, regardless of whether at idle or not. As such, if there isn't any excess to be had, there's no need to try and figure out how to make use of it.

On the other hand, the computational effort usually for an AI self-driving car does go upward as the driving situation gets more and more complicated. The AI "cognitive" workload for a self-driving car that's in the middle of a busy downtown city street, involving dozens of pedestrians, a smattering of bicycle riders, human driven cars that are swooping here and there, and the self-driving car is navigating this at a fast clip, along with maybe not having ever traversed this road before, and so on, it's quite a chore to be keeping track of all of that.

The AI self-driving car was presumably outfitted with sufficient computational resources to handle the upper peak loads (it better be!). At the less than peak loads, and at the least workload times, there is usually computational resources that are not being used particularly. It's those "available" resources that we're saying could be used. As stated earlier, it's not a must have. At the same time, as the case was made herein, it certainly could be some pretty handy icing on the cake.

The next time that you find yourself sitting at a red light and thinking about the weekend BBQ coming up, please make sure to keep a sufficient amount of mental resources aimed at the driving task. I don't want to be the person that gets bumped into by you, simply because you had grilled burgers and hot dogs floating in your mind.

CHAPTER 12
HURRICANES AND
AI SELF-DRIVING CARS

CHAPTER 12

HURRICANES AND
AI SELF-DRIVING CARS

Living in Southern California means that it is best to be prepared for the possibility of earthquakes. Some say we are the earthquake capital of the country, though this is a debatable assertion. Some of my colleagues from other parts of the U.S. seem to think that we have earthquakes constantly and that I'm unable to walk outside of my home or office without staggering along due to the ground shaking. Not quite, or at least not due to earthquakes.

For my colleagues along the Atlantic, we tend to trade barbs about earthquakes versus hurricanes.

Which is better or worse, the earth shaking or a torrent of wind, rain, and floods? Neither one is desirable, but some say that at least a hurricane you usually know beforehand that it is coming, while an earthquake tends to just suddenly appear. Hurricanes seem to cast a wider and larger path of destruction than does an earthquake. Both a hurricane and an earthquake are measured on scales of magnitude, and I think we all realize not all hurricanes are of the same ferocity and likewise not all earthquakes are of the same bone shaking impact.

In the case of earthquakes, we have the famous Richter scale as a measure of an earthquake and it handily provides a mathematical means to quantify the nature of the earthquake, doing so by using the seismograph and analyzing the amplitude of the waves detected. The moment an earthquake hits, people are instantly wondering what Richter score it is. There's even at times a bit of bravado about having experienced a higher Richter score than someone else has.

Perhaps less well-known is the hurricane metric which is referred to as the Saffir-Simpson Hurricane Wind Scale (SSHWS), which most people don't know the name of the metric but they likely know about the categories of hurricanes that it depicts. The least impactful hurricane gets into category 1, while the worst hurricane gets into category 5. Some people at times say that a hurricane is so terrible that it is a category 6, but this is not considered a valid category and meant to allude to the notion that the hurricane is essentially off-the-scale, so to speak.

Note that the SSHWS is only a measure of wind speed. It does not include the amount of rain involved, and nor does it have any aspect about flooding included into it. Those that defend the use of the SSHWS suggest that the simplicity of it is what makes the metric easy to use and describe. Were it to include other factors, the metric might become confusing or difficult to express. Generally, it seems that we all assume that a higher SSHWS score is likely to be accompanied by more rains and more flooding, and thus by an informal account we tend to encompass more than just the wind into the scale.

Category 1 is a hurricane that is considered the least intrusive and tend to produce minor damages more than true structural damages. Weak trees can be toppled over. Roof tiles can go flying. Relatively minor coastal flooding might occur. Power outages usually are spotty. One must keep in mind though that even a category 1 can be lethal. The damage can be widespread and people can definitely get injured and killed during the storm.

Category 2 involves quite dangerous winds that can yank off roofs. Trees that are in good shape can nonetheless by torn from the ground and tossed around. Mobile homes often get severely damaged. Power outages can be large scale and the availability of proper drinking water can become a problem for local inhabitants.

Category 3 consists of very devastating damages. Flooding often becomes a significant issue associated with the high winds involved.

Power losses can last for days, weeks, or even months.

Category 4 is even worse and consists of catastrophic damages. Flooding can reach to the inland areas and all sorts of buildings and other manmade structures can be flattened.

Category 5 is the topmost range of the scale and consists of overwhelming damages. Besides massive flooding, there can also be tons of debris that is carried along by the waters. There's most likely power outages and drinkable water issues that will be a long-lasting problem for the residents of the areas impacted. Health consequences following the storm can be of great concern, including the possibility for the spreading of disease and other adverse health aspects.

You might be aware of Hurricane Florence, which recently hit the Carolinas and became the first major hurricane for the Atlantic 2018 hurricane season. Initial concerns were that it would land as a possible Category 4, and later it turned out to be a Category 1, though let's not minimize the damage that it brought forth. There were mandatory evacuation orders issued by North Carolina, South Carloina, and Virginia that encompassed mainly various coastal areas. With heavy rains, Florence dumped rain onto major roads and there were highways that were impassable due to flooding. In some areas, the rainfall measured 30 inches or more.

After the main brunt of Florence had struck, it was interesting to see the headlines about the storm, which proclaimed that the deadliest place to be post-Florence was on the roads. Analyses suggested that nearly half of the deaths due to Florence were in some manner related to cars. People either got caught in their cars while there was flooding and perished, or they were in their cars and got into deadly crashes due to the weather conditions. Included were situations of a falling trees that struck upon cars and ended-up killing the occupant inside the vehicle.

Studies by the National Hurricane Center seem to show that the number of deaths involved in hurricanes are not attributed solely to a hurricane while it is in its active state. Instead, about half of the deaths of a hurricane occur during the actual storm event and the other half occurs post-event. Thus, even if you manage to survive the hurricane itself, you need to be aware that there are still dangers afoot and that deaths can occur afterward. When you have flooded roads, power lines laying on the streets, trees drooping that are ready to fall over, tons of debris everywhere, it is a recipe for quite serious car-related incidents.

Speaking of cars, let's turn now toward the notion of how cars are integral to what people do when a hurricane is known to be on its way.

Let's consider three stages of a hurricane:

- Pre-hurricane

- Hurricane event

- Post-hurricane

For each of the stages, there are uses of cars that are relatively predictable.

During the pre-hurricane stage, people have usually been notified that a hurricane is coming. The general path and geographic reach of the hurricane is forecasted. The severity is guessed at. People are told to get prepared for the hurricane.

Some people will opt to make a stand and fight out the hurricane, while others will choose to leave the potential impacted area. Some will try to go to spots that might be less impacted or that are strengthened to hopefully deal with the hurricane. In some instances, government officials will suggest an evacuation of various areas or even possibly impose a mandatory order to evacuate.

If you were to focus just on the car use during the pre-hurricane stage, I'd assert that the use of cars is likely to go up in the geographical area because people are driving to get supplies for making their stand against the hurricane, or they are gathering up loved ones to try and make a stand together, etc.

Car use also would likely be going up as people opt to drive to an area that might be less impacted, or drive to a place that has strengthened shelters.

For those that opt to leave, they will use their cars to get to other places, often far away from the forecasted location of the hurricane. This might also entail the use of the cars for long distance driving, more so than most would normally be driving their cars. If you routinely drive your car around town, this escape effort might involve driving much greater distances.

If there is an urged evacuation, either one considered voluntary or one that is considered mandatory, the number of cars on the road can get quite large. Furthermore, the cars will likely be on the roads at the same time and often going in the same direction. In other words, it's not as though the cars are going any which way and randomly getting onto the roads, but instead the cars will tend to get bunched up as people take the same major arteries and are leaving at about the same day and times as others.

That covers much of the car use during the pre-hurricane stage.

Once the hurricane event gets underway, people might still try to use their cars. It could be that they have a change of heart and decide to now try and evacuate. It could be that they discover that a loved one is in jeopardy, and so they decide to brave the storm and drive to that person. They themselves might need medical care as a result of the storm underway and try to drive to a hospital or medical facility accordingly.

The car traffic is likely quite sparse in comparison to the pre-hurricane situation. But, the weather conditions are likely much worse. This complicates the driving task. Cars might not be able to cope with flooding. A car might hit debris and become disabled. Pounding rain and the high winds might make it nearly impossible to see what's up ahead of the car. And so on.

For the post-hurricane, there is likely to be once again a massive movement of cars, presumably as people opt to drive back to their neighborhoods. They don't quite bunch up in the same manner as when they evacuated, but there is a likely high volume of cars, and all headed back into their respective towns. At this point, bridges might be out, roads might be closed, and the path to get around could be quite convoluted.

The post-hurricane driving might seem tempting to do. The storm has passed, and so people probably think it is "safe" to drive again. But, this is perhaps deceiving. In addition to the lousy driving conditions of the roadways, you are also likely to have drivers that are emotionally distraught and caught somewhat off-guard by the soured conditions of the roads. The chances of car incidents might tend to rise as people are contending with the road conditions and the circumstances of the overall destruction wrought by the hurricane.

What does this have to do with AI self-driving cars?

At the Cybernetic AI Self-Driving Car Institute, we are developing AI software for self-driving cars. One aspect of AI self-driving cars is their ability to cope with "extraordinary" driving situations, such as driving tasks that might occur related to a natural disaster such as a hurricane.

Many of the auto makers and tech firms that are developing AI self-driving cars are so busy with getting self-driving cars to drive under everyday road conditions that they consider dealing with circumstances of natural disaster related driving to be an edge problem. An edge problem in the computer field is one that you consider to be at the edge of what you are otherwise trying to solve. It is not considered core.

Those AI developers faced with getting self-driving cars to drive around on nice dry roads in pristine weather conditions are already overburdened trying to make that happen. Dealing with the situations of having roads that are covered in debris, well, that's a secondary problem. Coping with heavy rains and high winds, that's a secondary problem. In short, they assume that once they can get the "normal" driving aspects figured out, they'll then look into dealing with the "extreme" driving situations.

Another aspect to be aware of involves the levels of self-driving cars. The topmost level is considered Level 5. A Level 5 self-driving car is one that can be driven by the AI as though it is the same as if a human driver was driving the car. Indeed, there is not a human driver present in a Level 5 self-driving car because one is not needed. Even if a human driver opted to go in a Level 5 self-driving car, there usually is no provision for a gas pedal, nor a brake pedal, nor a steering wheel, since these are contraptions used by human drivers. For AI self-driving cars less than a Level 5, a human driver must be present and is considered responsible for the driving of the car. This though creates issues since there is then a co-sharing of the driving task between the AI and the human driver.

For purposes herein, I'm going to focus solely on the Level 5 self-driving car. I'd like to be able to take you through the aspects of how the AI might deal with the hurricane aspects involved in the driving task. That being said, I'd like to also mention that once we have self-driving cars that are at say the Level 3 and Level 4, it is going to be dicey as to how those self-driving cars are used during these kinds of natural disasters. You are looking at a potential "struggle" between what the human driver believes should be done during the driving and versus what the AI on-board is asserting should be done. For today's discussion, let's put that aside on aim at the all-AI and only-AI driving aspects involved in Level 5 self-driving cars.

Some pundits for AI self-driving cars are apt to suggest that the AI for a Level 5 self-driving car is going to do a better job at driving than human drivers, and they extend this same logic to the circumstances involving natural disaster such as hurricanes. This seems like quite an over-simplification and not readily something that can be considered verifiable when you consider the matter at-hand.

First, let's start with the pre-hurricane driving tasks.

Suppose there is a mass exodus of cars, all tending to head on the same roads and heading in the same direction, doing so at roughly the same day and times. For human drivers, this is essentially like a snarled freeway commute when everyone is headed to work at the same time and on the same freeways.

It is presumed that the AI self-driving cars will improve these snarls by being able to communicate and coordinate with each other. Via the use of OTA (Over The Air) and V2V (vehicle to vehicle communications), the self-driving cars will electronically convey where they are going and be able to interact with other self-driving cars on the road. This could reduce the friction associated with today's human drivers that often are inflexible and unyielding to other drivers and as a result presumably it causes things to get botched up.

The notion of having only AI self-driving cars on the roadways is a key assumption that these pundits tend to make. I'd like to point out that in the United States alone there are 200+ million conventional cars. Those conventional cars are not going to magically become AI self-driving cars. Instead, there will be a likely gradual reduction in the number of conventional cars, doing so slowly, commensurate with the advent of AI self-driving cars becoming prevalent.

In short, I'd predict that we are going to have a mixture of human driven cars and AI self-driving cars for many years to come. Perhaps for many decades. Some might even resist giving up the "privilege" of driving (some could argue it is a "right"), and it isn't clear cut if we'll even ultimately have only AI self-driving cars on the roadways. Others argue that maybe human driven cars will be restricted in terms of where they can drive and when they can drive, thus allowing for our roads to be "devoted" exclusively to true AI self-driving cars. This is a public debate topic, for sure.

So, in terms of a mass evacuation order due to a pending hurricane, in some Utopian world it might be the case that only AI self-driving cars are undertaking the driving task and thus they all coordinate with each other. This could ease some aspects of the driving. But, also keep in mind that if you only have a two-lane road and you try to put thousands upon thousands of cars on it, the coordination and communication is not necessarily going to lead to all of those self-driving cars zooming along at maximum speeds. The clog factor will come to play.

Meanwhile, in any case, it is more likely you'll have a mixture of human driven cars and AI self-driving cars mixed into the exodus. This will tend to reduce the coordination aspects among the many cars involved. You are likely to still have car incidents, including human driven cars hitting AI self-driving cars, and AI self-driving cars hitting human driven cars. This also raises the issue of how to deal with an AI self-driving car that's been involved in a car incident, which might render the AI unable to further drive the car, whereas a human might have been able to further maneuver a conventional human driven car.

On a related topic, the question arises as to how the AI will opt to undertake the driving task when confronted with the actual hurricane conditions.

Suppose you've decided that you are hunkering down at your home, hoping to outlast the vicious storm. As the hurricane descends upon your neighborhood, you have second thoughts about trying to holdout in your home. So, you jump in your car and desperately now seek to escape the storm, even though you are smack dab in the middle of it.

A human driver might be willing to take some pretty risky efforts while driving a car in such a situation. That road up ahead looks partially flooded, but is it so flooded that it cannot be utilized? It's the only way out-of-town and perhaps worth the risk of driving onto it. The alternative is that you try to retreat back to your home, but that doesn't seem like a good alternative either. You must choose between the proverbial rock and a hard place.

Some pundits of AI self-driving cars would say that the AI should always take the least risky approach and always drive solely in a legal manner. That is again some kind of utopian world. In the real-world, the driver of a car often has to make some very tough decisions. If the AI were to detect that there is water on the roadway, but not able to gauge how deep it is, should the AI just flat out refuse to attempt to drive through the water?

If you say yes, the AI should refuse, but as I've just described, the scenario is that you either take a chance to drive on the flooded street or you go back to your home that might become demolished by the storm. It's not an easy decision to make. If the AI is going to be the grand arbitrator, it seems unlikely that it can make these kinds of driving decisions since it is only "aware" of the obstacles ahead, and even in this case the AI is "unsure" of how severe an obstacle it really is.

You might say that we can "solve" this dilemma by merely asking the human occupant what is to be done. AI self-driving cars are going to have various conversational capabilities to converse with the occupants in the self-driving car. All the AI has to do is ask the humans that are inside the car, should it proceed ahead into the flooded street, and it might also aid their thinking process by pointing out that there is water there and the car could get stuck in the water.

This idea of asking the human occupants opens another can of worms.

Suppose you've put your children into the AI self-driving car and decided that you'll stay at the house but that you want your children to now escape from the storm. The AI then is going to ask the children to make this kind of potential life or death decision. Maybe not advisable.

You could say that the parent staying at the home could call the AI of the self-driving car and tell it what to do, but this presumes that an electronic communication is viable, and I'd bet that under the storm conditions of hurricane you aren't likely to get much of a connection.

Let's suppose there were adults in the AI self-driving car and that the AI asked those adults about what to do. One of the adults says go back to the house, while the other adult says to proceed forward onto the flooded street. What does the AI do now? I am sure there are some pundits that would say there needs to be determined beforehand an adult that is the "owner" and outweighs any other adults that might be present. I assure you this is another rabbit hole that we can descend into without much end to it.

For a true Level 5 AI self-driving car, I think that we need to consider the aspect that the AI is going to need to make these kinds of decisions, though doing so is not easy and indeed quite problematic. Imagine if you had a human chauffeur driving the car. What would that person do? Sure, they might listen to other adults in the car and so on, but in the end, they are at the driving wheel and they make the final decision. In some respects, we're going to have to figure out how the AI can do this, if it truly is going to be considered the driver of the car.

You can repeat all of the aforementioned considerations when it comes to the post-hurricane driving situation. Cars that come back after a hurricane are bound to confront flooded streets, heavy debris, trees nearly fallen over, etc. The AI needs to somehow consider the risk factors in all of these driving conditions and then figure out where to drive and how to drive.

Consider too that the AI self-driving car has cameras, radar, LIDAR, sonic, and other such sensors for purposes of detecting the roadway conditions. If you have rain coming down, it can adversely impact those sensors in terms of what they can detect. If there are heavy winds and items are rapidly blowing back-and-forth along the streets, this is difficult to detect and track. Suppose too that it is nighttime, and the electrical power is out, thus there are no street lights and no background lighting emanating from nearby buildings and homes. These further obscure the roadway and impair the driving task.

For those of you that cling to the notion that the AI is going to be a better driver than a human, I'd suggest you consider how well the AI can drive in these kinds of adverse conditions and compare it to a human. You might right away say that humans have problems driving in these conditions and get into road accidents accordingly. You are right. But, if you think that the AI can somehow miraculously also drive in these kinds of conditions and not get into a car incident, you have no idea what the reality of the sensors and the AI systems are able to achieve.

It is quite possible and even probable that an AI self-driving car in these conditions could readily get struck by flying debris and get into some kind of highway difficulties.

The AI self-driving car might not detect a weakness upcoming in the roadbed ahead and fall right into a morass that opens up.

Water on the roadway might appear to be a thin layer, and once the AI drives into the middle of an intersection, it gets stuck because the water is much deeper there.

On and on, there are plentiful ways in which the AI self-driving car is going to get into trouble. Yes, just as a human would. But, the point is that it cannot necessarily drive better than a human could in these situations. Some pundits seem to have a robot-like romantic notion in their minds that the AI can discern all roadway conditions completely, but that's just not practical.

I'll return to an earlier point that some would make, namely that the AI should have "enough sense" that it doesn't get itself into these kinds of binds. It won't have to make these tough decisions since it won't allow itself to get into these situations.

That doesn't make any sense per se.

As the example about staying home versus getting on the road illustrates, are you suggesting that if the AI receives let's say electronic weather reports that tell it is unsafe to drive on the roads, the AI should then refuse to allow the self-driving car to be used?

I'd dare say that you'd have likely as many people killed or injured when forced to not be able to use their cars, as you would by having the AI self-driving car proceed. Of course, we don't know for sure what the numbers would show, since we have no ready way to compare the idea of having cars that won't go versus cars that will go (currently, it's up to the judgment of the human car drivers).

You cannot narrowly look at the number of deaths due to roadway incidents associated with hurricanes and magically declare those deaths would not have happened if we only had AI self-driving cars.

We need to be realistic and estimate how many deaths could still have happened due to the AI self-driving car driving in such conditions. And, we would need to somehow include the deaths that might have occurred because the AI self-driving cars refused the human requests to drive them (perhaps getting stuck then in their homes and getting killed by the storm that strikes their home), if that's how we as a society want the AI system to act.

I realize there's another side of that same coin. If people falsely believe that the AI is magical and can drive in tough situations that we know it cannot readily do so, those people might be inclined to go ahead and try to have the AI drive out of a hurricane or get involved in AI driving journeys that might otherwise have been judged as too dangerous.

You might say to the AI, let's get going, and suppose it cautions that the weather bureau says don't drive, but that if the human insists then the AI will go ahead and try.

That's an equally bad situation perhaps as the circumstance of the AI being insistent that it won't drive period.

When you are the driver of a car, you hopefully tend to temper whether to drive as based on how well you think you can drive in the roadway conditions being faced.

Some might be deluded into believing that the AI can get them out of any jam, and thus choose to use the AI self-driving car in a natural disaster when it would have been better had they not done so.

It's a conundrum.

You can likely also see why there are auto makers and tech firms that see this as an edge problem.

You might say it is at the edge because it rarely comes up, but that's not really quite true because if you add together all of the different types of natural disasters, including hurricanes, tornados, earthquakes, floods, tsunamis, avalanches, mudslides (we have those in SoCal!), it comes out to a lot of circumstances involving the same kinds of hard choices for the AI and driving aspects that are very thorny.

That's more so why it is perhaps being considered an edge problem.

Having to deal with the numerous contemptuous aspects about the driving task in the context of a natural disaster is much more complicated than aiming at an AI self-driving car that can drive you to work each day and drive you home, doing so on pristine roads in pristine weather conditions.

Some would say that we need to have AI self-driving cars that can walk before they can run, and thus keep the scope of the problem narrowed to the more mundane and straightforward driving situations.

I assure you, it's not going to be long before we need to have AI self-driving cars that can step-up to handling the driving tasks involving natural disasters. I've used hurricanes herein as an exemplar. As they say, for AI self-driving cars that are oriented only to the straightforward driving situations, we aren't in Kansas anymore and need to think further outside the box.

CHAPTER 13

OBJECT VISUAL TRANSPLANTS

AND

AI SELF-DRIVING CARS

CHAPTER 13

OBJECT VISUAL TRANSPLANTS
AND
AI SELF-DRIVING CARS

Have you ever seen the videos that depict a scene in which there is some kind of activity going on such as people tossing a ball to each other and then a gorilla saunters through the background? If you've not seen any such video, it either means you are perhaps watching too many cat videos or that you've not yet been introduced to the concept of inattentional blindness or what some also consider an example of selective attention.

The gorilla is not a real gorilla, but instead a person in a gorilla suit (wanted to mention this in case you were worried that an actual gorilla was invading human gatherings and that the planet might be headed to the apes!). Overall, the notion is that you become focused on the other activity depicted in the video and fail to notice that a gorilla has ambled into the scene. When I tell people about this phenomenon, and if they've not yet seen one of these videos, they are often quite doubtful that those viewing such videos really did not see the gorilla.

Of course, now that I've told you about it, you are not likely to be "fooled" by any such video since you have been forewarned about it. Sorry about that. Guess I should have said *spoiler alert* before I told you about the gorilla.

In any case, for those doubters about the assertion that people watching such a video are apt to not notice a gorilla (which, not noticing a squirrel might seem more plausible, I acknowledge), I assure you that a large number of cognition related experiments have been done with the "invisible gorilla" videos and such studies support this claim. The experiments well-document that many people watching the video are completely unaware that a gorilla moseyed into the scene.

In fact, if you ask such people immediately after viewing the video whether they noticed a gorilla, most people swear it is outright impossible that a gorilla was in the scene. Upon showing them the video a second time, they then see the gorilla, but also insist that you are tricking them by showing an identical video but one that you've sneakily inserted a gorilla into after-the-fact. These people will be utterly convinced that you are trying to trick them into falsely believing that the original video had a gorilla in it.

One experiment even involved videoing the person as they initially watched the gorilla related video, so that after being told about the gorilla, the person could watch the video of themselves watching the video, and hopefully then believe that there was a gorilla in the initial video. I'm sure that there are some so suspicious that they figure you doctored the video of the video and thus refuse to still believe what they saw (or, what they didn't see).

There is a bit of trickery somewhat involved in this matter. Most of the time, the experimenter tells the person to be watching for something else in the video, such as watching to see if anyone drops the ball while tossing it or counting how many times the ball is tossed back-and-forth. I mention this rather important point because if you had no other focus related to the video, the odds are much higher that you would notice the gorilla. Because your attention has been purposely shaped though by the experimenter, you tend to block out other aspects that don't pertain to the matter you were directed to pay attention to.

From a cognitive perspective, the aspect of not noticing the gorilla is at times attributed to inattentional blindness. This means that you were not particularly paying attention to spot the gorilla and were therefore blind to noticing it. Others tend to describe this as an example of selective attention. Your attention is focused on something else that you were instructed to watch for. As a result, you select just those aspects in the scene that are related to the needed focus. No need to watch for other aspects and in fact it could be distracting if you did look elsewhere in the scene and therefore you might end-up doing worse on the assigned task at-hand.

Let's switch now from talking about gorillas to instead talking about elephants.

You've likely heard the famous expression about there being an elephant in the room. This is a popular metaphorical idiom and means that there is something that everyone notices or is aware of, but for which no one wants to bring it up or talk about it. For example, I went to an evening party the other night and one of the attendees arrived wearing a quite unusual hat. The attendees were all exceedingly reserved and civil, and no one overtly pointed at the hat or made any direct explicit remarks about the hat. The hat was the elephant in the room. It was there but no one particularly spoke of it. We all saw it and knew that it was unusual.

This summer, I went to our local county fair and was able to stand in a room with an elephant. Yes, an actual elephant. In this case, everyone knew there was an elephant in the room and everyone spoke up about it and pointed at it. This was not a metaphorical elephant. Though, it certainly would have been more interesting if the elephant had been in the room and everyone pretended to not notice. I guess that might be somewhat dangerous though, if the elephant suddenly decided to lumber around in the room.

Anyway, some AI researchers recently conducted a fascinating study about an elephant in a room (of sorts). It was a picture of an elephant. The experiment they conducted dealt with the use of Machine Learning (ML) and artificial neural networks (ANN).

Allow me to elaborate.

First, you might be aware that when using Machine Learning and deep neural networks that you need to contend with so-called adversarial examples. This refers to the notion that some ML and ANN's can be hyper-sensitive to targeted perturbations.

Let's suppose you opt to train a neural network to be able to find images of turtles. Little turtles, big turtles, turtles hiding in their shells, turtles poking their heads out, etc. You start by showing the neural network hundreds or maybe thousands of relatively crisp and clear-cut pictures of turtles. The neural network seems to gradually be getting pretty good at picking out the turtle in the pictures being shown to it. You test this by showing the neural network a picture that has a turtle and a squirrel, and sure enough the neural network is able to spot which of those animals is the turtle (and doesn't misidentify the squirrel as being a turtle).

Great, you are ready to use the neural network. But, suppose I do a bit of photoshop work on the picture that contained the turtle and the squirrel. I make a copy of the squirrel's tail and paste it onto the posterior of the turtle. I copy one of the legs of the turtle onto the squirrel. Admittedly, this looks somewhat Frankenstein-like, but go with me on this notion for the moment.

I show the picture to the neural network. What could happen is that the neural network now reports that the turtle is not a turtle and asserts that there is not a turtle at all in the picture. Or, the neural network could assert that there are two turtles in the picture, falsely believing that the squirrel is also a turtle. How could this happen?

Sometimes, even a small perturbation can confuse the neural network. If the neural network was focusing on only the legs of turtles, and it detected a turtle leg on the squirrel, it might then conclude that the squirrel is also a turtle. If the neural network had been honing on the tail of the turtle to determine whether a turtle is a turtle, the aspect that the turtle had a squirrel's tail would have caused the neural network to no longer believe that the turtle is a turtle.

This is one of the known dangers, or let's say inherent limitations, about the use of machine learning and neural networks. A good AI developer will try to ascertain the sensitivity of the neural network to the various "factors" that the neural network had landed upon to do its detective work. Unfortunately, many deep neural networks are so complicated that it is not readily feasible to determine what it is using to do the detective work. All you have is a complicated set of mathematical aspects and for which you might not be able to "logically" discern what it refers to.

I've mentioned many times that this is something that AI self-driving cars need to be attune to. There are various studies that have shown how easy it can be to confuse a machine learning algorithm or neural network that might be used by an AI self-driving car. These are often used when the AI is examining the visual camera images being collected by the sensors of the self-driving car.

For several of my articles about notable machine learning and neural network limitations and concerns related to AI self-driving cars, see these:

At the Cybernetic AI Self-Driving Car Institute, we are developing AI software for self-driving cars. As such, we are actively using and developing these AI systems via the use of machine learning and neural networks. It's important for the auto makers and tech firms to be using such tools carefully and wisely.

Allow me to elaborate.

First, I'd like to clarify and introduce the notion that there are varying levels of AI self-driving cars. The topmost level is considered Level 5. A Level 5 self-driving car is one that is being driven by the AI and there is no human driver involved. For the design of Level 5 self-driving cars, the auto makers are even removing the gas pedal, brake pedal, and steering wheel, since those are contraptions used by human drivers. The Level 5 self-driving car is not being driven by a human and nor is there an expectation that a human driver will be present in the self-driving car. It's all on the shoulders of the AI to drive the car.

For self-driving cars less than a Level 5, there must be a human driver present in the car. The human driver is currently considered the responsible party for the acts of the car. The AI and the human driver are co-sharing the driving task. In spite of this co-sharing, the human is supposed to remain fully immersed into the driving task and be ready at all times to perform the driving task. I've repeatedly warned about the dangers of this co-sharing arrangement and predicted it will produce many untoward results.

Let's focus herein on the true Level 5 self-driving car. Much of the comments apply to the less than Level 5 self-driving cars too, but the fully autonomous AI self-driving car will receive the most attention in this discussion.

Here's the usual steps involved in the AI driving task:

- Sensor data collection and interpretation
- Sensor fusion
- Virtual world model updating
- AI action planning
- Car controls command issuance

I've mentioned earlier in this discussion that one aspect to be careful about involves the potential of adversarial examples to confuse or mislead the AI system. There's another somewhat similar potential difficulty involving what is sometimes called object transplants.

A recent study undertaken by researchers at York University and the University of Toronto provides an insightful analysis of the concerns related to object transplanting (the study was cleverly entitled "The Elephant in the Room"). Object transplanting can be likened to my earlier comments about the gorilla in the video, though with a slightly different spin involved.

Imagine if you were watching the video that had a gorilla in it. Suppose that you actually noticed the gorilla when it came into the scene. If the scene consisted of people tossing a ball back-and-forth, would you be more likely to believe that it was a real gorilla or more likely to believe it is a fake gorilla (i.e., someone in a gorilla suit)? Assuming that the people kept tossing the ball and did not get freaked out by the presence of the gorilla, I'd bet that you'd mentally quickly deduce that it must be a fake gorilla.

Your context of the video would remain pretty much the same as prior to the introduction of the gorilla. The appearance of the gorilla did not substantially alter what you thought the scene consisted of. Would the introduction of the gorilla cause you to suddenly believe that the people must be in the jungle someplace? Probably not. Would the gorilla cause you to start looking at other objects in the room and begin to think those might be gorilla related objects?

For example, suppose there was in the room a yellow colored stick. Before the gorilla appeared, you noticed the stick and just assumed it was nothing more than a stick. Once the gorilla arrived, if you are now shifting mentally and thinking about gorilla's, maybe the yellow stick now seems like it might be a banana. You know that gorillas like bananas. Therefore, something that has a somewhat appearance of a banana, might indeed be a banana.

I realize you might scoff at the idea that you would suddenly interpret a yellow stick to be a banana simply because of the gorilla being there. A child watching the video might be more susceptible to making that kind of mental leap. The child has perhaps not seen as many bananas in their lifetime as you have, and thus a yellow stick might seem visually close enough to the resemblance of a banana that a child would mistake it for such. The child didn't think it was a banana before seeing the gorilla, it was the gorilla that caused the child to re-interpret the scene and the stick-like object in the context of a gorilla being there.

Visual object transplanting can impact the detection aspects of a trained machine learning system such as a convolutional deep neural network in a potentially similar way.

Using the popular Tensorflow object detection capability, and when combined with the Microsoft MS-COCO dataset, the researchers used a picture of a human sitting in a room and playing video games, and then did some object transplanting into the picture to see what the neural network would report about the objects in the picture (essentially, the researchers were doing a photoshop style transformation to the picture).

They transplanted an image of an elephant so that it appears in the picture with the sitting human. In some instances, the neural network did not detect that the elephant was in the picture, presumably not even noticing that it was there (thus, the clever titling of the research study as dealing with the elephant in the room!).

Depending upon where the elephant was positioned in the picture, the neural network at one point reported that the elephant was actually a chair. In another instance, the elephant was placed near to other objects that had been earlier identified, such as cup and a book, and yet the neural network no longer reported having found the cup or the book. There were also instances of switched identifies, wherein the neural network had identified a chair and a couch, but with the elephant nearby to those areas of the picture, the neural network then reported that the chair was a couch and the couch was a chair.

You might complain about this experiment and say that it is perhaps "unfair" to suddenly place an elephant into a picture that has nothing to do with elephants. The neural network had not been explicitly trained to have a co-occurrence of an elephant and the sitting human playing a video game. Well, the researchers considered this aspect and repeated the experiment but used a picture for which they merely took items already in the picture and moved those selected items around the scene. Once again, there were various inappropriate results produced by the neural network involving object misidentifications of one kind or another.

I would also suggest that we should decidedly not have much sympathy for the neural network per se and the aspect that it had not been trained on the co-occurrence possibilities – it's inherent inability to readily cope with the co-occurrence aspects "on the fly" so to speak is a weakness that we must overcome overall for such AI systems.

On a related note, I've previously mentioned in the realm of AI self-driving cars that there has been an ongoing debate related to the same notion of object transplanting, specifically the topic of a man on a pogo stick that suddenly appears in the street and near to an AI self-driving car.

There are some AI developers that have argued that it's understandable that the AI of a self-driving car might not recognize a man on a pogo stick that's in the street. By recognize, I mean that the visual images captured by the self-driving car are examined by the AI and that the AI system was not able to discern that the object in the street consisted of a man on a pogo stick. It detected that an object was there, and had a rather irregular shape, but it was not able to discern that the shape consisted of a person and a pogo stick (in this instance, the two are combined, since the man was on the pogo stick and pogoing).

Why would it be useful or important to discern that the shape consisted of a person on a pogo stick?

You, as a thinking human being, and assuming that you've seen a pogo stick before, and one that's in use, you likely know that it involves going up-and-down and also moving forward or backward or side-to-side. If you were driving along and suddenly saw a person pogoing in the street, you'd likely be cognizant that you should be watching out for the potential erratic moves of the pogo stick and its occupant. You could potentially even predict which way the person was going to go, by watching their angle and how hard they were pogoing.

An AI system that merely construes the pogoing human as a blob would not readily be able to predict the behavior of the blob. Predictions are crucial when you drive a car. Human drivers are continually looking around the surroundings of the car and trying to predict what might happen next. That bike rider in the bike lane might be weaving just enough that you are able to predict that they will swerve into your lane, and so you take precautionary measures in-advance. We must expect AI self-driving cars, and especially the true Level 5 self-driving cars, must be able to do this same kind of predictive modeling.

The range of potential problems associated with object transplanting woes includes:

- In the case of object transplanting, there is the chance that the transplanted object is not detected at all, even though it might normally have been detected in some other context.

- Or, the confidence level or probability attached to the object certainty might be lessened in comparison to what it might otherwise have been (in the case of the elephant added into the picture and the subsequent missing cup or book, it could be that the neural network had detected the cup and the book but had assigned a very low probability to their identities, and so reported that they weren't there, based on some threshold level required to be considered present in the picture).

- The detection of the transplanted object, if detection does occur, might lead to misidentification of other objects in the scene.

- Other objects might no longer be detected.

- Or, those other objects might have a lessened probability assigned to them as identifiable objects. There can be both local and non-local effects due to the transplanted object.

- Other objects might get switched in terms of their identities, due to the introduction of the transplanted object.

For AI self-driving cars, there are a myriad of sensors that collect data about the world surrounding the self-driving car. This includes cameras that capture pictures and video, it includes radar, it includes sonic, it includes LIDAR, and so on. The AI needs to examine the data and try to ferret out what the data indicates about the surrounding objects. Are those cars ahead of the self-driving car or are they motorcycles? Are there pedestrians standing at the curb or just a fire hydrant and a light post? These are crucial determinations for the AI self-driving car and its ability to perform the driving task.

AI developers need to take into account the limitations and considerations that arise due to object transplanting. The AI systems of the self-driving car need to be shaped in a manner that they can sufficiently and safely deal with object transplantation and do so in real-time while the self-driving car is in motion. The scenery around the self-driving car will not always be pristine and devoid of unusual or seemingly out-of-context objects.

When I was a professor, each year a circus came to town and the circus animals arrived via train, which happened to get parked near the campus for the time period that the circus was in town. A big parade even occurred involving the circus performers marching the animals from next to the campus and over to the nearby convention center. It was quite an annual spectacle to observe.

I mention this because among the animals were elephants, along with giraffes and other "wild" animals. Believe it or not, on the morning of the annual parade, I would usually end-up driving my car right near to the various animals as I was navigating my way onto campus to teach classes for the day. It was as though I had been transported to another world.

If I was using an AI self-driving car, one wonders what the AI might have construed of the elephants and giraffes that were next to the car. Would the AI have suddenly changed context and assumed I was now driving in the jungle? Would it get confused and believe that the light poles were actually tall jungle trees?

I say this last aspect about the circus in some jest but do want to be serious about the facet that it is important to realize the existing limitations of various machine learning algorithms and artificial neural network techniques and tools. AI self-driving car makers need to be on their toes to prepare for and contend with object transplants. And that's no elephant joke. That's the elephant in the room and on the road ahead for AI self-driving cars.

APPENDIX

APPENDIX A
TEACHING WITH THIS MATERIAL

The material in this book can be readily used either as a supplemental to other content for a class, or it can also be used as a core set of textbook material for a specialized class. Classes where this material is most likely used include any classes at the college or university level that want to augment the class by offering thought provoking and educational essays about AI and self-driving cars.

In particular, here are some aspects for class use:

o   <u>Computer Science</u>. Studying AI, autonomous vehicles, etc.

o   <u>Business</u>. Exploring technology and it adoption for business.

o   <u>Sociology</u>. Sociological views on the adoption and advancement of technology.

Specialized classes at the undergraduate and graduate level can also make use of this material.

For each chapter, consider whether you think the chapter provides material relevant to your course topic. There is plenty of opportunity to get the students thinking about the topic and force them to decide whether they agree or disagree with the points offered and positions taken. I would also encourage you to have the students do additional research beyond the chapter material presented (I provide next some suggested assignments they can do).

RESEARCH ASSIGNMENTS ON THESE TOPICS

Your students can find background material on these topics, doing so in various business and technical publications. I list below the top ranked AI related journals. For business publications, I would suggest the usual culprits such as the Harvard Business Review, Forbes, Fortune, WSJ, and the like.

Here are some suggestions of homework or projects that you could assign to students:

a) <u>Assignment for foundational AI research topic</u>: Research and prepare a paper and a presentation on a specific aspect of Deep AI, Machine Learning, ANN, etc. The paper should cite at least 3 reputable sources. Compare and contrast to what has been stated in this book.

b) <u>Assignment for the Self-Driving Car topic</u>: Research and prepare a paper and Self-Driving Cars. Cite at least 3 reputable sources and analyze the characterizations. Compare and contrast to what has been stated in this book.

c) <u>Assignment for a Business topic</u>: Research and prepare a paper and a presentation on businesses and advanced technology. What is hot, and what is not? Cite at least 3 reputable sources. Compare and contrast to the depictions in this book.

d) <u>Assignment to do a Startup:</u> Have the students prepare a paper about how they might startup a business in this realm. They must submit a sound Business Plan for the startup. They could also be asked to present their Business Plan and so should also have a presentation deck to coincide with it.

You can certainly adjust the aforementioned assignments to fit to your particular needs and the class structure. You'll notice that I ask for 3 reputable cited sources for the paper writing based assignments. I usually steer students toward "reputable" publications, since otherwise they will cite some oddball source that has no credentials other than that they happened to write something and post it onto the Internet. You can define "reputable" in whatever way you prefer, for example some faculty think Wikipedia is not reputable while others believe it is reputable and allow students to cite it.

The reason that I usually ask for at least 3 citations is that if the student only does one or two citations they usually settle on whatever they happened to find the fastest. By requiring three citations, it usually seems to force them to look around, explore, and end-up probably finding five or more, and then whittling it down to 3 that they will actually use.

I have not specified the length of their papers, and leave that to you to tell the students what you prefer. For each of those assignments, you could end-up with a short one to two pager, or you could do a dissertation length paper. Base the length on whatever best fits for your class, and the credit amount of the assignment within the context of the other grading metrics you'll be using for the class.

I mention in the assignments that they are to do a paper and prepare a presentation. I usually try to get students to present their work. This is a good practice for what they will do in the business world. Most of the time, they will be required to prepare an analysis and present it. If you don't have the class time or inclination to have the students present, then you can of course cut out the aspect of them putting together a presentation.

If you want to point students toward highly ranked journals in AI, here's a list of the top journals as reported by *various citation counts sources* (this list changes year to year):

o   Communications of the ACM

o   Artificial Intelligence

o   Cognitive Science

o   IEEE Transactions on Pattern Analysis and Machine Intelligence

o   Foundations and Trends in Machine Learning

o   Journal of Memory and Language

o   Cognitive Psychology

o   Neural Networks

o   IEEE Transactions on Neural Networks and Learning Systems

o   IEEE Intelligent Systems

o   Knowledge-based Systems

GUIDE TO USING THE CHAPTERS

For each of the chapters, I provide next some various ways to use the chapter material. You can assign the tasks as individual homework assignments, or the tasks can be used with team projects for the class. You can easily layout a series of assignments, such as indicating that the students are to do item "a" below for say Chapter 1, then "b" for the next chapter of the book, and so on.

a) What is the main point of the chapter and describe in your own words the significance of the topic,

b) Identify at least two aspects in the chapter that you agree with, and support your concurrence by providing at least one other outside researched item as support; make sure to explain your basis for disagreeing with the aspects,

c) Identify at least two aspects in the chapter that you disagree with, and support your disagreement by providing at least one other outside researched item as support; make sure to explain your basis for disagreeing with the aspects,

d) Find an aspect that was not covered in the chapter, doing so by conducting outside research, and then explain how that aspect ties into the chapter and what significance it brings to the topic,

e) Interview a specialist in industry about the topic of the chapter, collect from them their thoughts and opinions, and readdress the chapter by citing your source and how they compared and contrasted to the material,

f) Interview a relevant academic professor or researcher in a college or university about the topic of the chapter, collect from them their thoughts and opinions, and readdress the chapter by citing your source and how they compared and contrasted to the material,

g) Try to update a chapter by finding out the latest on the topic, and ascertain whether the issue or topic has now been solved or whether it is still being addressed, explain what you come up with.

The above are all ways in which you can get the students of your class involved in considering the material of a given chapter. You could mix things up by having one of those above assignments per each week, covering the chapters over the course of the semester or quarter.

As a reminder, here are the chapters of the book and you can select whichever chapters you find most valued for your particular class:

Companion Book By This Author

Advances in AI and Autonomous Vehicles: Cybernetic Self-Driving Cars

Practical Advances in Artificial Intelligence (AI) and Machine Learning

by

Dr. Lance B. Eliot, MBA, PhD

This title is available via Amazon and other book sellers

Lance B. Eliot

226

<u>Companion Book By This Author</u>

Self-Driving Cars:
"The Mother of All AI Projects"

by Dr. Lance B. Eliot, MBA, PhD

This title is available via Amazon and other book sellers

Companion Book By This Author

Innovation and Thought Leadership on Self-Driving Driverless Cars

by Dr. Lance B. Eliot, MBA, PhD

This title is available via Amazon and other book sellers

This title is available via Amazon and other book sellers

Companion Book By This Author

Introduction to
Driverless Self-Driving Cars

by Dr. Lance B. Eliot, MBA, PhD

Chapter Title

This title is available via Amazon and other book sellers

<u>Companion Book By This Author</u>

Autonomous Vehicle Driverless Self-Driving Cars and Artificial Intelligence

by Dr. Lance B. Eliot, MBA, PhD

This title is available via Amazon and other book sellers

***Transformative Artificial Intelligence
Driverless Self-Driving Cars***

by Dr. Lance B. Eliot, MBA, PhD

This title is available via Amazon and other book sellers

Companion Book By This Author

Disruptive Artificial Intelligence and Driverless Self-Driving Cars

by Dr. Lance B. Eliot, MBA, PhD

Chapter Title

This title is available via Amazon and other book sellers

<u>Companion Book By This Author</u>

State-of-the-Art
AI Driverless Self-Driving Cars

by Dr. Lance B. Eliot, MBA, PhD

<u>Chapter Title</u>

This title is available via Amazon and other book sellers

Companion Book By This Author

Top Trends in
AI Self-Driving Cars

by Dr. Lance B. Eliot, MBA, PhD

This title is available via Amazon and other book sellers

Companion Book By This Author

AI Innovations
and Self-Driving Cars

by Dr. Lance B. Eliot, MBA, PhD

This title is available via Amazon and other book sellers

Companion Book By This Author

Crucial Advances for
AI Self-Driving Cars

by Dr. Lance B. Eliot, MBA, PhD

Chapter Title

This title is available via Amazon and other book sellers

Companion Book By This Author

Sociotechnical Insights and AI Driverless Cars

by Dr. Lance B. Eliot, MBA, PhD

Chapter Title

This title is available via Amazon and other book sellers

Companion Book By This Author

Pioneering Advances for AI Driverless Cars

by Dr. Lance B. Eliot, MBA, PhD

This title is available via Amazon and other book sellers

Companion Book By This Author

Leading Edge Trends for AI Driverless Cars

by Dr. Lance B. Eliot, MBA, PhD

This title is available via Amazon and other book sellers

ABOUT THE AUTHOR

Dr. Lance B. Eliot, MBA, PhD is the CEO of Techbruim, Inc. and Executive Director of the Cybernetic Self-Driving Car Institute, and has over twenty years of industry experience including serving as a corporate officer in a billion dollar firm and was a partner in a major executive services firm. He is also a serial entrepreneur having founded, ran, and sold several high-tech related businesses. He previously hosted the popular radio show *Technotrends* that was also available on American Airlines flights via their in-flight audio program. Author or co-author of a dozen books and over 400 articles, he has made appearances on CNN, and has been a frequent speaker at industry conferences.

A former professor at the University of Southern California (USC), he founded and led an innovative research lab on Artificial Intelligence in Business. Known as the "AI Insider" his writings on AI advances and trends has been widely read and cited. He also previously served on the faculty of the University of California Los Angeles (UCLA), and was a visiting professor at other major universities. He was elected to the International Board of the Society for Information Management (SIM), a prestigious association of over 3,000 high-tech executives worldwide.

He has performed extensive community service, including serving as Senior Science Adviser to the Vice Chair of the Congressional Committee on Science & Technology. He has served on the Board of the OC Science & Engineering Fair (OCSEF), where he is also has been a Grand Sweepstakes judge, and likewise served as a judge for the Intel International SEF (ISEF). He served as the Vice Chair of the Association for Computing Machinery (ACM) Chapter, a prestigious association of computer scientists. Dr. Eliot has been a shark tank judge for the USC Mark Stevens Center for Innovation on start-up pitch competitions, and served as a mentor for several incubators and accelerators in Silicon Valley and Silicon Beach. He served on several Boards and Committees at USC, including having served on the Marshall Alumni Association (MAA) Board in Southern California.

Dr. Eliot holds a PhD from USC, MBA, and Bachelor's in Computer Science, and earned the CDP, CCP, CSP, CDE, and CISA certifications. Born and raised in Southern California, and having traveled and lived internationally, he enjoys scuba diving, surfing, and sailing.

ADDENDUM

Leading Edge Trends for AI Driverless Cars

Practical Advances in Artificial Intelligence (AI) and Machine Learning

By
Dr. Lance B. Eliot, MBA, PhD

For supplemental materials of this book, visit:

www.ai-selfdriving-cars.guru

For special orders of this book, contact:
LBE Press Publishing
Email: LBE.Press.Publishing@gmail.com

www.ingramcontent.com/pod-product-compliance
Lightning Source LLC
Chambersburg PA
CBHW051228050326
40689CB00007B/838